D0461257

PRAYING
★★★★ WITH THE ★★★★
PRESIDENTS

Our Nation's Legacy of Prayer

RON DICIANNI

Praying With the Presidents
ISBN 1-59185-408-3
Copyright © 2004 by Ron Dicianni
Cover Illustration copyright © Ron Dicianni
Black and white graphics of the presidents used by permission of Bartleby.com, Inc.

Requests for information may be addressed to:

The children's book imprint of Strang Communications Company
600 Rinehart Rd., Lake Mary, FL 32746
www.charismakids.com

Unless otherwise noted, all Scripture is taken from the New King James Version of the Holy Bible,
copyright © 1982 by Thomas Nelson, Inc. Used by permission.
Scripture noted NIV is taken from the New International Version® of the Holy Bible, © 1973, 1978,
1984 by International Bible Society. Used by permission of Zondervan Publishing House.

All rights reserved.

CharismaKids is a trademark of Strang Communications Company.

Children's Editor: Pat Matuszak
Designer: Joe DeLeon

Printed in China
04 05 06 07/ LP / 5 4 3 2 1

DEDICATION

As always to the Lord Jesus Christ whose sacrifice and blessing gives us something worth writing and painting about.

With gratitude to our editor Pat Matuszak, whose skill, support, and ability to gently motivate without nagging made this possible. Thanks for all the times you've gone to bat for our project.

Finally, to the leaders of this country who have continued to remember that they need God. I pray we never see the day where presidents feel that they are able to govern on their own.

Every author needs help from a good assistant. Mine came from the best. Not only a skilled researcher and writer, but far more to me as my son, I proudly give my thanks to you, Grant. In you, God gave me a skilled craftsman, as found in the temple artisans in the Book of Exodus. Yours were with words, and a fine wordsmith you are! You held my arms up when they were tired, just as Aaron and Hur did for Moses. I thank God for you.

———————————— ★ ————————————

Authors' Note: In regard to the personal lives of certain presidents, the authors feel the need to add a comment. Some made choices that might call into question their suitability for inclusion in a book of this nature. While we in no way condone these questionable and morally suspect actions, we choose not to use them as the basis of a conclusion against the men who made them. What is important is the action weighed against each man's decision to try to live a Christian life. Man is a fallen creature and each of us has made decisions that to some extent may call into question our fitness to proclaim our Christianity. While they may have failed, we believe absolutely that Jesus' death is sufficient to grant forgiveness for any act to anyone who asks for it. Each of the presidents in question publicly or privately acknowledged regret for his actions and we as authors will leave the decision of their fate up to God. We seek only to show that even those presidents whose conduct was questionable, still found it absolutely essential to appear in the presence of the Almighty on bended knee and ask direction for the nation. They say that there are no atheists in foxholes. Likewise, we have found the same axiom holds true for those individuals who find themselves in the heat of battle in the White House.

FUN FACTS TO KNOW ABOUT OUR PRESIDENTS

To find out more, go to each president's page...

1st President: George Washington
The words "So help me God" were Washington's own addition to the presidential oath of office.

2nd President: John Adams
Adams was the first president to live in the White House.

3rd President: Thomas Jefferson
He died just hours before his longtime rival, John Adams, on Independence Day, July 4, 1826.

4th President: James Madison
James Madison was one of the "Fathers of the Constitution" who signed the Declaration of Independence.

5th President: James Monroe
His Monroe Doctrine stated that European countries should not continue to take over land in the Western Hemisphere.

6th President: John Quincy Adams
John Quincy Adams was the son of the nation's second president, John Adams.

7th President: Andrew Jackson
He was the first president to ever travel by railroad and the first to have been a prisoner of war before he came to office.

8th President: Martin Van Buren
Van Buren was the first president to be born in the formalized United States of America.

9th President: William Henry Harrison
Harrison contracted pneumonia and died in office. He served the shortest term as president.

10th President: John Tyler
On Tyler's last day in office he invited Texas to join the United States.

11th President: James Knox Polk
He hosted the first White House Thanksgiving, and news of his nomination was carried over the newly invented 'telegraph' system as one of the first news flashes sent all over the country.

12th President: Zachary Taylor
He was elected president when he had never voted—not even for himself!

13th President: Millard Fillmore
Fillmore started the first library in the White House.

14th President: Franklin Pierce
He once gave a three-thousand-word speech from memory.

15th President: James Buchanan
Buchanan had been a diplomat to Russia and England.

16th President: Abraham Lincoln
Lincoln was the tallest president (six feet, four inches), and the first president to wear a beard.

17th President: Andrew Johnson
Johnson's vice presidency came as a surprise because he and Lincoln were from opposite parties. Lincoln chose someone from the opposite side to help unite the country.

18th President: Ulysses S. Grant
"U.S." Grant was originally named Simpson Ulysses Grant, but his initials were switched in a clerical error. He liked his name better that way and changed his signature.

19th President: Rutherford B. Hayes
He was the winner of a very confusing election that had to be decided by appointing an Electoral Commission.

20th President: James A. Garfield
He was the last of the "log cabin" presidents who were born on the frontier. He was also a minister who preached revival messages.

21st President: Chester A. Arthur
One of the jobs he had before becoming president was teaching in an elementary school.

22nd & 24th President: Grover Cleveland
He was the first president to be married in office and also the first to appear in a movie, *A Capital Courtship*. But it did not make President Cleveland a movie star!

23rd President: Benjamin Harrison
He won the presidency away from Grover Cleveland. He lost it back to him again four years later.

25th President: William McKinley
He died after he was shot while shaking hands with a crowd at the World's Fair in Buffalo.

26th President: Theodore Roosevelt
The stuffed children's toy—the 'Teddy Bear'—was named after him and his love for wildlife. He also established the national forests and parks.

27th President: William Howard Taft
After he left office as president, he was appointed Chief Justice of the United States, a position he held for the rest of his life.

28th President: Woodrow Wilson
A learning disability made reading difficult for him, so he taught himself to remember everything he saw, even if he'd only seen it one time.

29th President: Warren Harding
He was the first president to be broadcast over the radio. In fact, he was the first president to even own a radio!

30th President: Calvin Coolidge
He asked thirty reporters to meet him in a high school classroom in South Dakota, then handed each reporter a slip of paper that simply said that he would not run for president again.

31st President: Herbert Hoover
He was president during the Great Depression and gave all his salary to charity and public service.

32nd President: Franklin Delano Roosevelt
He was the only president to serve three terms in a row—that's twelve years.

33rd President: Harry S. Truman
Truman had a lot of catching up to do as the new president after FDR died. Truman had not known about the development of a new super weapon called the atomic bomb.

34th President: Dwight D. Eisenhower
Disneyland opened and NASA was created while Ike was president.

35th President: John F. Kennedy
President Kennedy was both the youngest president elected and the youngest president assassinated.

36th President: Lyndon B. Johnson
He worked on a road construction crew and taught in a high school before going into politics.

37th President: Richard M. Nixon
Neil Armstrong's 'one small step' onto the surface of the moon happened during his presidency.

38th President: Gerald R. Ford
Ford was the only president to have been an Eagle Scout.

39th President: Jimmy Carter
He professed his faith in God on a PBS television program.

40th President: Ronald Reagan
At the age of 69, he was the oldest man to be elected president.

41st President: George H.W. Bush
He was awarded the Distinguished Flying Cross as a navy pilot.

42nd President: William J. Clinton
He played the saxophone well enough to have considered a career as a musician.

43rd President: George W. Bush
He served as managing general partner of the Texas Rangers baseball team before becoming Governor of Texas.

George Washington

BORN February 22, 1732, in Westmoreland County, Virginia
1ST PRESIDENT 1789–1797

—————— ★ ——————

As a young man of barely twenty, Washington sat down before a writing table lit by candlelight and wrote these words with a quill pen into his prayer journal…

"I beseech thee, my sins, remove them from thy presence, as far as the east is from the west, and accept of me for the merits of thy son Jesus Christ, that when I come into thy temple, and compass thine altar, my prayers may come before thee as incense; and as thou wouldst hear me calling upon thee in my prayers, so give me grace to hear thee calling on me in thy word, that it may be wisdom, righteousness, reconciliation and peace to the saving of the soul in the day of the Lord Jesus. Grant that I may hear it with reverence, receive it with meekness, mingle it with faith, and that it may accomplish in me, Gracious God, the good work for which thou has sent it."

Think About This President and Prayer
George Washington asked God to hear his prayer. How did he ask God to speak back to him?

What did he ask God to do in his heart so that he could receive wisdom?

How to Pray Like George Washington
"Lord, give me this day the wisdom to obey Your Word. I know that I have sinned and ask that You forgive me. I pray that You watch over me and my family and that You guide us each day. Help me to obey those in authority over me. Let me live my life in service to You and show Your salvation to those around me. Amen."

Scripture
"If my people, who are called by my name, will humble themselves and pray and seek my face and turn from their wicked ways, then will I hear from heaven and will forgive their sin and will heal their land."
2 Chronicles 7:14, NIV

History
On April 30, 1787, a formally dressed man wearing a white wig stood on a balcony before a multitude of spectators in the square in New York. America's first president asked for a Bible and humbly uttered the first words of a new presidency. Little did the crowd below know that these words were Washington's own addition to the oath of office; setting a precedent for those who followed: "So help me God."

George Washington has been a source of fascination since 1778, famous as a man, a general, and the first president of a new republic, the United States of America. Born in 1732 Washington was not predisposed by status toward challenging British rule. One of his first adventures as a teenager was to help map and survey the area of Shenandoah for Lord Fairfax. The life that he could expect was one typical of eighteenth century Virginia. He would be an area gentleman, manage his land, and engage in commerce. Many men in Washington's social class would become involved in local governance or the military and he was no exception. As an officer, Washington won acclaim in the Seven Years' War and would bring that experience to bear as he led his rag-tag collection of troops on to defeat the mightiest army of the time.

George Washington was the president of many 'firsts' for America. He was the first five-star general, the first president, the first commander-in-chief, and one of the founding fathers of this nation. The words of his farewell address ring true today when he proclaimed, "Reason and experience both forbid us to expect that national morality can exist apart from religious principle."

Think About This President and Prayer

When President Adams prayed for people who would live in the house after him, for whom was he praying?

This president wrote that Jesus Christ could do miracles today. Why did he say he believed that is true?

How to Pray Like John Adams

"Lord, I realize that there is no safety except the protection found in You. I pray that those who step foot in this house will see You reflected in my life. You are the Author of all creation and there is nothing You cannot do if I will only trust in You. Let me believe in the miracles of Your Son and His ultimate sacrifice on the cross. Amen."

Scripture

"The Lord shall preserve your going out and your coming in from this time forth, and even forevermore."
Psalm 121:8

History

John Adams, the country's second president faced some different issues than George Washington faced. Although he was still a trailblazer in what it meant to be president, many believe Adams was more of a philosopher than a politician. Adams was vice president under Washington and he was eager to take a larger responsibility. As an early patriot, John Adams used his law degree from Harvard to contribute to the success of independence as a delegate to both the First and Second Continental Congress. As president, Adams faced a growing rift in the American political consciousness. Instead of a united front against a common enemy, Americans were splitting along the ideology of the separate political parities.

A brief war with the French and the development of American naval prowess went a long way in pushing America forward in the ranks of world power. One great achievement of his presidency was the successful completion of the new presidential residence, now called the White House, which Adams occupied in November 1800, before it was even fully furnished.

The end of Adams' presidency came about when his rival and vice president, Thomas Jefferson, was elected. Amazingly, on his deathbed Adam's last words would be about Jefferson, who, unknown to Adams, had died just a few hours before.

John Adams

BORN October 30, 1735, in Braintree, Massachusetts
2ND PRESIDENT 1797–1801

★

On a blustery fall day, people huddled together to hear the second president's first speech in front of his new house:

"I pray Heaven to bestow the best of blessing on this house and on all that shall hereafter inhabit it. May not but honest and wise men ever rule under this roof!"
November 2, 1800—Dedication of the White House

Years before assuming the presidency, a youthful Adams wrote this statement of logic and faith into his school journal:

"The great and Almighty author of nature, who at first established those rules which regulate the world, can as easily suspend those laws whenever his providence see sufficient reason for such suspension. This can be no objection, then, to the miracles of Jesus Christ."
March 2, 1756—Journal Entry

Thomas Jefferson

BORN April 13, 1743, in Albermarle County, Virginia
3RD PRESIDENT 1801–1809

──────────── ★ ────────────

As a strong president, Jefferson was mindful of the dangers and stood before our elected officials and prayed:

"Endow with Thy spirit wisdom those whom in Thy Name we entrust the authority of government, that there may be justice and peace at home, and that through obedience to Thy law, we may show forth Thy praise among the nations of earth.

"In time of prosperity fill our hearts with thankfulness, and in the day of trouble, suffer not our trust in Thee to fail; all of which we ask through Jesus Christ our Lord, amen."
March 4, 1805—National Prayer for Peace

Think About This President and Prayer
Thomas Jefferson asked God to give wisdom to those in authority. What did he write would happen if the leaders were wise?

Where did President Jefferson want Americans to put their trust in "the day of trouble"?

How to Pray Like Thomas Jefferson
"Thank You, Lord, that I live in a free nation that allows me to express my faith. Help my leaders have wisdom to keep this nation free. Fill my heart with thankfulness and help me not to lose my trust in You during hard times. I praise You for freedom and ask that You help me to obey Your word and show others I serve You. I ask this in the name of our Lord, Jesus Christ. Amen."

Scripture
"Where then does wisdom come from? Where does understanding dwell? ...God understands the way to it and he alone knows where it dwells."
Job 28:20, 23, NIV

History
Thomas Jefferson is probably one of the best-known and most important founders of America. His writing ability was one of his strong talents. That ability propelled him to greatness when he helped write the Declaration of Independence. Born in 1743, Jefferson was the son of a landowner. He was trained as a lawyer and wrote often on many topics. His writings go beyond government or political subjects.

During the presidency of his political rival John Adams, Jefferson served as vice president. He won the election when running against Adams to become the next president. Jefferson's election firmly established the two-party system in America and showed the world that power could be justly transferred with out bloodshed. The other great accomplishment of his presidency was the addition of over three-quarters of a million acres. The Louisiana Purchase doubled the size of the country. Jefferson also focused on paying down the national debt and other economic policies to bolster the country's economy.

Following his term, Jefferson retired to his estate, Monticello, in Virginia, where he died just hours before his longtime rival, John Adams. Amazingly both men died in 1826 on the day Americans celebrate their independence, July 4th. He included these words of faith in the Declaration of Independence, one of the most powerful documents ever written: "...for the support of this Declaration, with a firm reliance on the protection of Divine Providence, we mutually pledge to each other our Lives, our Fortunes, and our sacred Honor."
Declaration of Independence—adopted July 4, 1776

Think About This President and Prayer
Who did James Madison say guards and guides the destiny of nations of the earth?

What did this president say people need to do first to be a good citizen or "member of civil society?"

How to Pray Like James Madison
"Every day is built on the foundation of Your love and power, Father God, not on my own abilities. Let me be a follower of Your Son first, and help me to make everything else second to that. My success is in doing Your will for my life. Help me to obey Your still, small voice in my heart each day. Amen."

Scripture
"What other nation is so great as to have their gods near them the way the Lord our God is near us whenever we pray to him?"
Deuteronomy 4:7, NIV

History
It might seem odd, but James Madison's greatest contribution was not in being the nation's fourth president. During his life many would argue that Madison was the "Father of the Constitution" to which he often protested that that document was in fact the collaboration of several people's work. He had become a respected and experienced political figure. Madison's presidency saw some of the greatest upheaval and events that the young country had ever witnessed.

During the presidency the nation rallied as French and British warships continued to ruin sea commerce. Confrontations at sea, aggravated by unsuccessful attempts to negotiate, led to the War of 1812. The British invaded America pushing as far south as Washington. They seized the capital and burned several important buildings. Madison's last years in office were spent recovering from the damage that had been caused by the war. He was aided by an American people thriving on a new sense of pride and nationalism after having defeated the world's strongest power. He stood at the nation's helm through political, national, and military hardships.

He retired to his property in Virginia where he died almost two decades after leaving office.

James Madison

BORN March 16, 1751, in Orange County, Virginia
4TH PRESIDENT 1809–1817

───────────── ★ ─────────────

James Madison was overjoyed at the success of the democracy he had helped to build. He felt honored to be elected the fourth president of the United States. In his first official speech he made it clear he felt God had guided the leaders of the new nation:
"We have all been encouraged to feel the guardianship, and guidance of that Almighty Being, whose power regulates the destiny of nations."
March 4, 1809—Inaugural Address

James Madison made the following argument against critics who had tried to limit religion through regulations. In a crowded meeting hall he thundered these words:
"Before any man can be considered a member of civil society, he must be considered as a subject of the Governor of the Universe."
June 1785—Memorial and Remonstrance Against Religious Assessments

James Monroe

BORN April 28, 1758, in Westmoreland County, Virginia
5TH PRESIDENT 1817–1825

★

As had his predecessors before him, Monroe stood in front of the White House and gave honor to the One who controls his nation's fate:

"I enter on the trust to which I have been called by the suffrage of my fellow citizens with my fervent prayers to the Almighty that He will be graciously pleased to continue to us that protection which He has already so conspicuously displayed in our favor."
March 4, 1817—First Inaugural Address

After two full terms as president, James Monroe again told the nation to remember that their blessings came from God:

"For these blessings we owe to Almighty God, from which we derive them, and with profound reverence, our most grateful and unceasing acknowledgements."
December 7, 1824—Eighth Annual Address

Think About This President and Prayer
James Monroe said his fellow citizens called him to be president by voting, but whom did he say gave him protection?

What does it mean to be grateful?

How to Pray Like James Monroe
"Dear Lord, thank You for every blessing You have poured out. Help me fulfill the purpose You have called me to. I trust in Your protection each day. I trust in Your guidance. Guide our nation and our president and let him look to You for each decision. Let our leaders rely on Your protection and seek Your will. Amen."

Scripture
"For You are my hope, O Lord GOD; You are my trust from my youth...I will praise You yet more and more."
Psalm 71:5, 14

History
James Monroe was the last of the founding fathers to be elected president. He was elected to the presidency by a landslide and was the only candidate to run for re-election unopposed in his second term. Representing the only viable party at the time, Monroe led the nation in the "Era of Good Feelings" when there was little political infighting among the leaders.

Monroe's accomplishments were aggressive and helped the nation's growth. Monroe supported the idea of western expansion, and wanted the borders of the country to go all the way to the Pacific. Monroe made a policy that became known as the Monroe Doctrine. It stated that none of the European Powers should continue try to take over land in the Western Hemisphere.

He stood by President Jefferson, and Jefferson spoke highly of his moral character. The nation grew strong and a new era began with factories providing new jobs and steamboats making travel across the country faster. After Monroe's second term, he followed George Washington's lead of stepping down without a third term.

Think About This President and Prayer
Does John Quincy Adams think that God watches what people are doing and saying?

According to this president, what age should people be to read the Bible?

How to Pray Like John Quincy Adams
"Lord, let me never believe that for a moment I am out of Your sight. I stand before You in all things. Forgive me for living my life believing that my actions are hidden from You. It is with fearless confidence that I hand over the control of my life, my family, and my nation to You. Amen."

Scripture
[Jesus said] *"You are already clean because of the word which I have spoken to you. Abide in Me, and I in you. As the branch cannot bear fruit of itself, unless it abides in the vine, neither can you, unless you abide in Me."*
John 15:3–4

History
John Quincy Adams was the son of the nation's second president, John Adams. It was the first such time that relatives held the highest office of the land. He and his generation of leaders were the sons of the revolutionaries. While they had not participated at the beginning of creation of this new country, they had seen their parents craft a nation and were eager to take over the helm.

John Quincy Adams was a leader whose ideas needed a strong popular following. His election began with controversy. No candidate in the 1824 election had received a majority of the vote, so the decision went to the Congress. They were the ones who decided the results and they chose Adams.

After his presidency, Adams was elected by his home district to the House of Representatives where he served as an influential and successful statesman until he collapsed on the very floor of the House while serving. He was the first president to hold public office after his presidential term ended.

John Quincy Adams

BORN July 11, 1767, in Braintree, Massachusetts
6TH PRESIDENT 1825–1829

When John Quincy Adams stood up in front of his fellow Americans to take the oath of office, he believed he was not just standing before men. He spoke of the presence of God and of heaven:

"I appear, my fellow citizens, in your presence and in that of Heaven to by the solemnities of religious obligation to the faithful performance of the duties allotted to me...

"With fervent supplications for His favor, to His overruling providence I commit with humble but fearless confidence my own fate and the future destinies of my country."
March 4, 1825—Inaugural Address

In the mind of John Quincy Adams there was no confusion about the place of God's Word in America or his personal life:

"I speak as a man of the world to men of the world, and I say to you, Search the Scriptures! The Bible is the book of all others, to be read at all ages, and in all conditions of human life."

Andrew Jackson

BORN March 15, 1767, in Waxhaw, South Carolina
7TH PRESIDENT 1829–1837

———————— ★ ————————

Hundreds gathered to get their first look at President Jackson and hear his first words to the nation. These words come at the end of Jackson's first speech as president:

"And a firm reliance on the goodness of that Power whose providence mercifully protected our national infancy, and has since upheld our liberties in various vicissitudes, encourages me to offer up my ardent supplications that He will continue to make our beloved country the object to His divine care and gracious benediction."
March 4, 1829—First Inaugural Address

Jackson answered the question of the role of faith in government with these words:

"The Bible is the Rock on which this Republic rests."

Think About This President and Prayer
Liberty means freedom. How did President Jackson think our country was kept free from being taken over by other countries when it was young?

What does Andrew Jackson say about the Bible?

How to Pray Like Andrew Jackson
"Lord, I pray that You will keep our country free by Your truth. In my life and action let me inspire the hearts of those around me to live for You. I pray for this nation and that You keep us looking to Your Word for guidance. Let me firmly rely on Your power each day. Amen."

Scripture
[Jesus said] *"Therefore whoever hears these sayings of Mine, and does them, I will liken him to a wise man who built his house on the rock: and the rain descended, the floods came, and the winds blew and beat on that house; and it did not fall, for it was founded on the rock."*
Matthew 7:24–25

History
Andrew Jackson's assent to the presidency was an unusual one. He complained about the previous election, which he felt that a conspiracy had caused him to lose. But he won the people's vote twice when he focused his campaign on his war record and popular support. Jackson was a national hero with strong Southern support. The way he was elected closely resembles modern-day election strategies for well-known heroes.

The first president since Washington to have served in the organized American military, Jackson had very little formal education but managed to lead the nation to a couple of milestones. Under his presidency the national debt was fully paid and a new political party (the Whigs) emerged.

Jackson the first president to have ever been a prisoner of war and the first to ever use the railroad. Jackson's strong use of the powers of the office have led many historians to call Jackson the first of the modern-day presidents.

Think About This President and Prayer
In both of these quotes, the president thanks God for the same thing. What is the last word in each quote?

Martin Van Buren uses two different names for God. What are they? Do you know a name for Jesus that has the word "peace" in it?

How to Pray Like Martin Van Buren
"In times of plenty and in times of want, I look to You God. Even in my most difficult times I know that You are there guiding me. Help me to walk in Your ways each day regardless of the world around me and grant me Your gracious protection and support. Amen."

Scripture
"I will lie down and sleep in peace, for you alone, O LORD, make me dwell in safety."
Psalm 4:8, NIV

History
Without doubt Martin Van Buren's close alliance with President Jackson was important to his career. Jackson fought hard with those who tried to block Van Buren's election. As a president, Martin Van Buren's term was spoiled by troubling financial issues. Trained as a lawyer, he held many state posts in New York and later several positions within Jackson's administration. Although he worked hard on economic problems of the country, it entered a period of financial hardship.

Another 'first' for the presidency, Van Buren was the first president to be born in the formalized United States of America. His lasting contribution was in the introduction of the term OK. Originally used during his election campaign to stand for his nickname "Old Kinderhook," it has now come to have the meaning we know to today as "all right." Van Buren lost re-election to the Whig party in 1840 and his loss symbolized the first national Whig political victory.

Martin Van Buren

BORN December 5, 1782, in Columbia, New York
8TH PRESIDENT 1837–1841

As a new president, Martin Van Buren's first words set the tone for the next four years. With care, Van Buren used them to turn his audience's attention to God:

"Beyond that I only look to the gracious protection of the Divine Being whose strengthening support I humbly solicit, and whom I fervently pray to look down upon us all. May it be among the dispensations of His providence to bless our beloved country with honors and with length of days. May her ways be ways of pleasantness and all her paths be peace!"
March 4, 1837—Inaugural address

When he knew he had not been re-elected, Van Buren used one of his last chances to capture the nation's attention by imparting these words at his last national address…

"Our devout gratitude is due to the Supreme Being for having graciously continued to our beloved country through the vicissitudes of another year the invaluable blessings of health, plenty, and peace."
December 5, 1840—Fourth Annual Message

William Henry Harrison

BORN February 9, 1773, in Berkley Plantation, Virginia
9TH PRESIDENT 1841–1841

★

It seems ironic that one of the shortest-lived presidencies can yield one of the strongest statements on prayer and reliance on God:

"I deem the present occasion sufficiently important and solemn to justify me in expressing to my fellow citizens a profound reverence for the Christian religion and a thorough conviction that sound morals, religious liberty, and a just sense of religious responsibility are essentially connected with all true and lasting happiness; and to that good Being who has blessed us by the gifts of civil and religious freedom, who watched over and prospered the labors of our fathers and has hither to preserved to us institutions far exceeding in excellence those of any other people, let us unite in fervently commending every interest of our beloved country in all future time."
March 4, 1841—Inaugural Address

Think About This President and Prayer
President Harrison talks about "sound morals" that bring lasting happiness. What are morals?

This president thanks God for watching over the fathers of our country. Can you think of a time you were thankful for God watching over your own family?

How to Pray Like William Henry Harrison
"Dear God, I am thankful to be able to come to You in prayer and for who You are and what You have done in my life. Each day You have watched over my family and me and guided the work of our hands. Let me always trust You every day for the rest of my life. Amen."

Scripture
"Let the beloved of the Lord rest secure in him....the one the Lord loves rests between his shoulders."
Deuteronomy 33:12, NIV

History
Although Harrison represented a major victory for his newly formed party, it was only for a short time. Many know Harrison as the president serving the shortest term ever. Famous as "Old Tip" for the Battle of Tippecanoe, many voted for Harrison based on his military service and subsequent popularity.

Harrison died of pneumonia. Some say it was because of his 105-minute-long inaugural speech in the cold. Others say it was because he went to the market for groceries and yet others blame it on his riding in an open-topped carriage shortly after the election. All of those stories have one thing is common: Harrison in the cold without proper clothing. The end result was a dead president, an untested vice president, and two very frustrated political parties.

Think About This President and Prayer

When President Tyler looked back over the country's history, what did he thank God for?

Can you think of three things that have happened in your life or to our nation to thank God for in the past year?

How to Pray Like John Tyler

"As I look back over what You have done in my past, Lord God, let me see it as a hope of what You will do in my future. Thank You for Your guidance in my life, my family and my nation. Whether life has been easy or hard, thank You for being there with me and hearing my prayer. Amen."

Scripture

"Trust in the Lord and do good; dwell in the land and enjoy safe pasture."
Psalm 37:3, NIV

History

Tyler was sometimes called "His Accidency" because after President Harrison died of pneumonia, Tyler, his vice president, took his place as the new president. Tyler was not as well known as Harrison. He had never run for the office of President. He had been put on the election ticket to "balance" it since he had different ideas than Harrison about how to run the country. It was felt more people would vote for Harrison if his vice president represented those with different views.

Tyler tried hard to make his presidency a success through difficulty. He had to work with advisors on his cabinet who were appointed by Harrison and did not agree with some of his ideas. He had personal tragedy when his wife died while he was in office. But his presidency saw the beginning of trade with China and a first attempt to annex the territory of Texas. On the first try, Tyler failed to get approval to annex Texas, but following the next election Congress agreed to the annexation. On Tyler's last day in office, Texas was made a state. John Tyler would later become significant when the first southern states seceded in 1861. He attempted to help the states reach a compromise without leaving the Union. That attempt failed, so he worked with others to create the Confederacy. He was elected to hold office in the Confederate Congress, but he died before he could serve.

John Tyler

BORN March 29, 1790, in Greenway, Virginia
10TH PRESIDENT 1841–1845

When he became president, few knew what to expect from Tyler. They must have been thankful to have the new leader point toward the heavens as his source of guidance…

"The world has witnessed its rapid growth in wealth and population, and under the guide and direction of the superintending Providence the developments of the past may be regarded but as the shadowing forth of the mighty future."

Having not been elected to another term, Tyler had one last opportunity to leave words of wisdom for the people. A cold winter day, fire roaring in the background, Tyler concludes his last national address with these words…

"We have continued cause for expressing our gratitude to the Supreme Ruler of the Universe for the benefits and blessings which our country, under His kind providence, has enjoyed during the past year."
December 4, 1844—Fourth Annual Message

James Knox Polk

BORN November 2, 1795, in Mecklenburg County, North Carolina
11TH PRESIDENT 1845–1849

★

James Polk boldly declared that the nation's leaders needed God's help. The people of his day respected him for this and agreed with him:

"In assuming responsibilities so vast I fervently invoke the aid of that Almighty Ruler of the Universe in whose hands are the destinies of nations and of men to guard this Heaven-favored land against the mischiefs which without His guidance might arise from an unwise public policy. With a firm reliance upon the wisdom of Omnipotence to sustain and direct me in the path of duty which I am appointed to pursue."
March 4, 1845—Inaugural Address

Polk believed God's hand made our nation prosperous and often made public pronouncement of it saying…

"that Divine Being who has watched over and protected our beloved country from its infancy to the present hour to continue His gracious benedictions upon us, that we may continue to be a prosperous and happy people."

Think About This President and Prayer
What did President Polk want Americans to know about God?

Can we ask for God's blessing on our country today?

How to Pray Like James Polk
"I rely on Your power, Jesus. I believe that You alone hold all authority. I ask You to direct my life. Put me on the path my life should take. Keep me from straying. Protect me against unwise people who seek to destroy our nation or my life. Your leading and protection are what allow our people to continue to be a prosperous and happy. Please stay with us always. Amen."

Scripture
"Blessed is the man who walks not in the counsel of the ungodly, nor stands in the path of sinners, nor sits in the seat of the scornful; but his delight is in the law of the Lord, and in His law he meditates day and night. He shall be like a tree planted by the rivers of water, that brings forth its fruit in its season, whose leaf also shall not wither; and whatever he does shall prosper."
Psalms 1:1–3

History
James Polk believed the idea of "Manifest Destiny." That means he wanted to expand the U.S. borders from the Atlantic Ocean to the Pacific Ocean. British and Mexican military forces were occupying some of the territories in between at that time. Because of this belief in Manifest Destiny and his feeling that countries other than the United States should not claim land or have political influence on this continent, President Polk sent U.S. troops to war with Mexico. Most of the northwestern and southwestern states were added to the Union because of these battles.

Polk's presidency saw many firsts. He hosted the first White House Thanksgiving, and news of his nomination was carried over the newly invented telegraph system. It was one of the first news flashes sent all over the country.

Many Americans were unhappy that Polk had led the country into war. He became ill during the end of his term and his political party did not nominate him for re-election. James Polk died in 1849 shortly after leaving office.

Think About This President and Prayer

President Taylor thanked God for blessing our country in spite of hard times. Can we still be thankful for God's blessings on our country even when bad things happen today?

Do you think Americans still understand God's power to protect our country as much as President Taylor felt they did in his time?

How to Pray Like Zachary Taylor

"Dear Lord, although life may be hard from time to time, You have always blessed and protected me. In times when our country faces hard times, we can look to You for protection and provision. Help us to live in peace in the middle of conflict, and look to You as our hope. Amen."

Scripture

"I have called upon You, for You will hear me, O God; incline Your ear to me, and hear my speech. Show Your marvelous lovingkindness by Your right hand, O You who save those who trust in You from those who rise up against them."
Psalm 17:6–7

History

Zachary Taylor surprised a lot of people when he was elected president because he had avoided speaking out publicly on any issue. In fact he never voted—not even for himself!

Zachary Taylor was not known for being bold in standing for his beliefs. He tried to compromise as much as possible and seemed to keep his belief in God from influencing his presidential decisions. President Taylor was afraid that the unity between our states would come to an end during his time as leader. At that time in American history, several issues including slavery were being argued about, causing the Northern states and Southern states to become angry with each other. They were fighting so much that the Southern states were ready to leave the Union and form their own country. They were ready for a civil war.

Taylor wanted to keep the states together. Although he was able to avoid open battle by threatening to personally lead the Union army against the Southern states, Taylor's success didn't last long. He became sick and died after serving only one year as president. In a strange coincidence, eleven years after Taylor's death, his son, Richard Taylor, fought as a general for the Southern states in the war his father tried so hard to avoid.

Zachary Taylor

BORN November 24, 1784, in Orange County, Virginia
12TH PRESIDENT 1849–1850

President Taylor made it very clear whom he trusted:

"It is a proper theme of thanksgiving to Him who rules the destinies of nations that we have been able to maintain amidst all these contests an independent and neutral position toward all belligerent powers."
December 4, 1849—Annual Message

Taylor relied on God's guidance and let his nation know:

"During the past year we have been blessed by a kind Providence with an abundance of the fruits of the earth, and although the destroying angel for a time visited extensive portions of our territory with the ravages of a dreadful pestilence, yet the Almighty has at length deigned to stay his hand and to restore the inestimable blessing of general health to a people who have acknowledged His power, deprecated His wrath, and implored His merciful protection."

Millard Fillmore

BORN January 7, 1800, in Cayuga County, New York
13TH PRESIDENT 1850–1853

———————— ★ ————————

Grieving the death of President Taylor, Fillmore spoke words of comfort and told the country where he found his strength:

"I rely upon Him who holds in His hands the destinies of nations to endow me with the requisite strength for the task."
July 9, 1850—After Taking the Oath of Office

"… join me in humble and devout thanks to the Great Ruler of Nations for the multiplied blessings which He has graciously bestowed…Our liberties, religious and civil, have been maintained, the fountains of knowledge have all been kept open, and means of happiness widely spread…greater than…any other nation. And while deeply penetrated with gratitude for the past, let us hope that His all-wise providence will so guide our counsels as that they shall result in giving satisfaction to our constituents, securing the peace for the country, and adding new strength to the united Government under which we live."
December 2, 1850—First Annual Message to Congress

Think About This President and Prayer
Can you find two times President Fillmore asked God for strength in his prayers?

What challenges do you face in your life that need God's strength?

How to Pray Like Millard Fillmore
"Lord, in any time of trial I can look to You as the Author of all things. You are a God who generously gives us everything we need. When I feel weak, I will remember that You give me Your strength and wisdom. I thank You for speaking to me and leading me, and I ask that you continue to guide me, my family, and our leaders in these times. Amen."

Scripture
"I can do all things through Christ who strengthens me….And my God shall supply all your need according to His riches in glory by Christ Jesus. Now to our God and Father be glory forever and ever. Amen."
Philippians 4:13, 19–20

History
Millard Fillmore was another president who rose to office because of an unfortunate death. Following Zachary Taylor who had struggled to hold the Union together in the middle of deep divisions between North and South, Fillmore stepped into leadership of our country at a very tense time.

Fillmore's early years were spent on the frontier lands in a log cabin. Many people point to his life as an example of "the American Dream," where hard work and determination can take a person from having nothing to having a very powerful position. In spite of his position as president, Fillmore was humble and refused honors and awards because he didn't think he deserved them.

Fillmore started the first library in the White House, which shows his appreciation for books and learning. After his term as president was over, he spent time as the head of the University of Buffalo.

Think About This President and Prayer
Do you think President Pierce's reminder of the ways God had protected our country in the past helped people trust God for the country's present situations?

Does remembering times God has answered your prayers give you more faith to trust Him for your future?

How to Pray Like Franklin Pierce
"Thank You, Lord, that when I am weak and tired You remain strong. I can trust that Your Spirit guides and directs each step I take. You have answered my prayers before, and I know You will hear me now. Help our country remember that we cannot trust in our army's weapons or power. Our security and peace comes from You alone. Please bring our nation back to the place where we can truly say, 'In God We Trust.' Amen."

Scripture
"Blessed is the nation whose God is the LORD, the people He has chosen as His own inheritance....No king is saved by the multitude of an army; a mighty man is not delivered by great strength."
Psalm 33:12, 16

History
Things were still very tense in our country when Franklin Pierce became president. Many different ideas among leaders and the people faced him. In addition to the national pressure, he had great personal trouble to face. A tragedy struck the Pierces when their eleven-year-old son, Benjamin, was killed in a railroad accident shortly after the election.

Franklin Pierce was a striking mix of highs and lows. For example, he once gave a three-thousand-word speech from memory, but by his second year of college he had the lowest grades of his class. One of the most shocking things about Pierce's presidency was that while he was in office, he was arrested for running over an old lady while riding a horse.

Government parties had taken sides on many issues and wanted the president to decide who was right. Pierce attempted to keep from joining sides, but everything he did made one or both parties mad at him. Pierce had made his party so mad by trying to stay "on the fence" that they did not ask him to run for president a second time.

Franklin Pierce

BORN November 23, 1804, in Hillsboro, New Hampshire
14TH PRESIDENT 1853–1857

Franklin Pierce may have had many questions in his mind as he took office, but his faith showed him where to find the answers:

"...under the guidance of a manifest and beneficent Providence the uncomplaining endurance...only surpassed by the wisdom and patriotic spirit of concession which characterized all the counsels of the early fathers....I can express no better hope for my country than that the kind Providence which smiled upon our fathers may enable their children to preserve the blessings they have inherited."
March 4, 1853—Inaugural Address

Pierce knew that dependence on God guaranteed the safety of the nation. Our security is provided by superhuman power, not armies and weapons.

"It must be felt that there is no national security but in the nation's humble acknowledged dependence upon God and His overruling providence."

James Buchanan

BORN April 23, 1791, in Cove Gap, Pennsylvania
15TH PRESIDENT 1857–1861

★

James Buchanan knew that his skill as a diplomat was not enough to bring healing to the deep divisions of the nation. He stood before America and called on the power of the greatest Healer and Diplomat:

"In entering upon this great office I must humbly invoke the God of our fathers for wisdom and firmness to execute its high and responsible duties in such a manner as to restore harmony and ancient friendship among the people of the several States and to preserve our free institutions throughout many generations."
March 4, 1857—Inaugural Address

Think About This President and Prayer

The nation was full of fighting during Buchanan's presidency so he prayed for God to heal and restore relationships. Have you ever seen people who need healing in their relationships with one another?

Can you name some ways that praying for healing can help stop fighting and bring unity?

How to Pray Like James Buchanan

"O Lord, help me never to doubt that in moments of trouble You alone stay constant. I cannot look to others or myself for healing but I must rely on Your Spirit, which has guided me this far. I humbly ask You to touch our nation and heal the issues which divide us. No matter how bleak it may look, You are in control. Amen."

Scripture

"Come, and let us return to the Lord; for He has torn, but He will heal us; He has stricken, but He will bind us up."
Hosea 6:1

History

Without a doubt Buchanan came on the scene at a time of national chaos. The political party system was breaking down, the nation was spinning out of control, and somehow James Buchanan was asked to lead them both.

Buchanan had been a diplomat to Russia and England, where he helped to keep good relationships between different countries. But in spite of his experience with helping different people work together, the problems in our country's government were too big, and it completely broke down.

If only they would have looked to God for healing as Buchanan had prayed, but it appears that they didn't. No one would agree on anything. The government couldn't make any decisions. Buchanan tried his best, but there was nothing he could do to bring them back together again.

The nation was falling apart and Congress in part blamed the president for his failure to bring healing. James Buchanan stood before an angry Congress, sweat beading on his brow, convinced that although the darkest hour may loom, God had never failed to provide. It was with that conviction that he boldly asserted: "When we compare the condition of the country at the present day with what it was one year ago at the meeting of Congress, we have much reason for gratitude to that Almighty Providence which has never failed to interpose for our relief at the most critical periods of our history."

After his presidency was over, Buchanan retired to Pennsylvania. The country continued to spin out of control.

Think About This President and Prayer

Abraham Lincoln said he prayed because he felt like he had nowhere else to go for help. Tell about a time you felt like you needed help.

How can prayer and reading God's Word help guide you in situations when you don't know what to do?

How to Pray Like Abraham Lincoln

"Thank You for Your Word and its power. In moments of confusion let me find wisdom in its pages. Thank You for prayer, Lord Jesus. When I am weak let me find Your strength on my knees in prayer. You are always here for me, even when I feel like I have nowhere else I can turn. I live my life to praise You and to give thanks for Your goodness and power. Amen."

Scripture

"Your word is a lamp to my feet and a light to my path. You are my hiding place and my shield; I hope in Your word."
Psalm 119:105, 114

History

Outside of George Washington, Abraham Lincoln is probably the best known, most often quoted and most loved president. The country saw some of its hardest times and greatest accomplishments under the same man. By the end of President Lincoln's first term, the hope of solving our nation's problems was becoming strong.

Lincoln was the tallest president (six feet, four inches), and the first president to wear a beard. He grew up in log cabins in the Midwest and lacked formal education, but learned things by experience and hard work. He taught himself to become a lawyer and tried to run for political office in Illinois. He was defeated several times but he kept on trying. He was nicknamed "Honest Abe" and once wrote that he held honesty in high regard. His honesty and determination paid off when he was elected as president in 1861. He faced some of the hardest times our country has ever endured. Many feel that his greatest accomplishment as president was working on an amendment to the Constitution, that outlawed slavery.

Shortly after the end of the Civil War, on April 14, 1965, John Wilkes Booth shot Lincoln while he watched a performance at Ford's Theatre. The president died the following morning. Many people wonder what other great things a man like Lincoln could have done had he lived. However, what he did accomplish has won him the respect of many generations of Americans.

Abraham Lincoln

BORN February 12, 1809, in Hodgenville, Kentucky
16TH PRESIDENT 1861–1865

───────── ★ ─────────

Abraham Lincoln showed his deep-rooted faith by praying for God's wisdom on his knees. When we are tested, our true beliefs are revealed. President Lincoln humbly shows how his source of strength was not his armies or his skills, but his Savior:

"I have been driven many times to my knees by the overwhelming conviction that I had absolutely no other place to go."

Lincoln also lays out his opinion of the Bible in a very direct statement…

"I believe the Bible is the best gift God has ever given to man. All the good from the Savior of the world is communicated to us through this book."

Andrew Johnson

BORN December 29, 1808, in Raleigh, North Carolina
17TH PRESIDENT 1865–1869

★

So many have talked about God on their deathbed, just moments before seeing Him face-to-face. What greater tribute then in the final moments of life to be able to proclaim with confidence, as Andrew Johnson did, that…

"I have performed my duty to my God, my country, and my family. I have nothing to fear in approaching death. To me it is the mere shadow of God's protecting wing . . . Here I will rest in quiet and peace beyond the reach of calamity's poisoned shaft, the influence of envy and jealous enemies, where treason and traitors of State, backsliders and hypocrites in Church can have no peace."
Shortly before Johnson's death on July 31, 1875

Think About This President and Prayer
How do Andrew Johnson's prayers show us that he knew he would spend eternity in heaven with Jesus?

If you have asked Jesus to forgive your sins and accepted Him as Lord of your life, you will go to heaven when you die. Do you know where you will spend eternity?

How to Pray Like Andrew Johnson
"Lord, I come first and foremost to thank You. I thank You for Jesus' sacrifice on the cross for my sins and for His resurrection, which promises me eternal life in heaven with You when I die. I look forward to the day when I will see You face-to-face. Help me to show that truth to the world around me. Amen."

Scripture
"Therefore we also, since we are surrounded by so great a cloud of witnesses, let us lay aside every weight, and the sin which so easily ensnares us, and let us run with endurance the race that is set before us, looking unto Jesus, the author and finisher of our faith, who for the joy that was set before Him endured the cross, despising the shame, and has sat down at the right hand of the throne of God."
Hebrews 12:1–2

History
Thrust into leadership at the unbelievable moment of Lincoln's death, Andrew Johnson inherited a nation in distress. The South lay in ruin and the nation's symbol of unity and strength had just been assassinated. Johnson's vice presidency had come as a surprise to many because he and Lincoln were from opposite parties. Lincoln had specifically chosen someone from the opposite side of government to be his partner. He hoped this would help unite the country for the election of 1864. However, five days after his re-election, an assassin's bullet killed Abraham Lincoln and propelled Johnson to the presidency.

President Johnson's first and most troubling question was how to go about rebuilding the country, which had been destroyed by the Civil War. It was such a hard job that he did not want to run for re-election when his presidential term was over.

After his term, Johnson returned to Tennessee where he rejoined the Senate in 1875. He died shortly after being elected.

Think About This President and Prayer
What were some ideas during Grant's time that might have gone against what God instructs in His Word?

Have you ever had to make a choice between what people wanted you to do and what God instructs in His Word? What did you do?

How to Pray Like Ulysses S. Grant
"Dear Lord, let me have patience for those I come into conflict with and show them Your love and mercy. Help me to do my part in making this world a place where You can be praised. Let me never listen to people who go against Your Word, and help me to be a good example to everyone around me. Amen."

Scripture
"The LORD is on my side; I will not fear. What can man do to me?...It is better to trust in the LORD than to put confidence in man. It is better to trust in the LORD than to put confidence in princes."
Psalm 118:6, 8–9

History
"U.S." Grant, as friends in West Point knew him, was originally named Simpson Ulysses Grant but due to a clerical error, the names were switched. He liked the flair of the initials U.S. so much that he adopted those initials into his signature.

Grant was the conquering military hero of the Civil War and favorite candidate of the Republican Party. Republicans saw in Grant a chance to get the country back on track and were shocked when he was elected as president by only a small number of votes. Many explain Grant's narrow win by noting that he was popular with the recently freed slaves who voted for him. This resulted in a lack of white southern votes. His inauguration parade however was the largest ever with over eight full Army divisions participating.

Grant was another president with humble backgrounds. He felt that everything he did prior to the Civil War was a failure. At the end of his life, Grant was involved in a failed business venture when he learned he had throat cancer. In an attempt to settle his debts he agreed to pen his memoirs. Those memoirs were successful and brought in almost a half million dollars but, unfortunately, Grant died in 1885 shortly after finishing the last page.

Ulysses S. Grant

BORN April 27, 1822, in Point Pleasant, Ohio
18TH PRESIDENT 1869–1877

———————— ★ ————————

Ulysses S. Grant stepped into the presidency not taking credit for past successes or responsibility for future healing of the nation. Instead he rested his calloused hands on the lectern in front of him, and with his words hanging in the sunshine, pointed to the power that could make the Union whole:

"In conclusion I ask patient forbearance one toward another throughout the land, and a determined effort on the part of every citizen to do his share toward cementing a happy union; and I ask the prayers of the nation to Almighty God in behalf of this consummation."
March 4, 1869—Inaugural address

For Grant, there was one duty above freedom, and that was his duty to God.

"No political party can or ought to exist when one of its cornerstones is opposition to freedom of thought and to the right to worship God..."
—Personal Memoirs of U.S. Grant

Rutherford B. Hayes

BORN October 4, 1822, in Delaware, Ohio
19TH PRESIDENT 1877–1881

★

Rutherford B. Hayes was elected president during one of the most confusing elections in American history. Hayes didn't let the unusual circumstances stop him from recognizing God's leadership. Speaking to the people at his inauguration, he finished by saying:

"Looking for the guidance of that Divine Hand by which the destines of nations and individuals are shaped, I call upon you Senators, Representatives, judges, fellow citizens here and everywhere to unite with me in an earnest effort…"
March 5, 1877—Inaugural Address

Think About This President and Prayer
Why do we need to remember that God is in control of our lives, our families, and even of our country?

Why is it a good idea to invite others to pray with us?

How to Pray Like Rutherford B. Hayes
"Everything I have comes from You, Lord. Forgive me for the times when I make the mistake of taking for granted Your blessings and guidance. Help me remember that You are in control and I can bring all of my needs to You. I do not have to worry when other people are upset about things that happen. I can have peace because I know You will take care of me. Let each of my days be lived in humility and love before You. Amen."

Scripture
"Be anxious for nothing, but in everything by prayer and supplication, with thanksgiving, let your requests be made known to God; and the peace of God, which surpasses all understanding, will guard your hearts and minds through Christ Jesus."
Philippians 4:6–7

History
Rutherford B. Hayes was the winner of a very confusing election. People were arguing about several of the electoral votes and a special team of men was formed to decide who would get the confusing votes. Hayes was given the votes on the condition that he make many changes in the South.

Once in office, Hayes showed himself to be a man of reform and dignity. He kept all of the conditions he made upon receiving the votes that won him the presidency. Many of Rutherford Hayes' decisions as president showed his belief in the equality of all people. He worked hard to promote a better standard of life for the still newly freed slaves. In addition he made several changes that allowed women more power in government.

In his State of the Union speech, Hayes pointed to God as the reason for the success of the nation:

"The members of the Forty-sixth Congress have assembled in their first regular session under circumstances calling for mutual congratulation and grateful acknowledgment to the Giver of All Good for the large and unusual measure of national prosperity which we now enjoy."

Following his term, Hayes stepped down and retired to his home, Spiegel Grove, in Ohio. He lived in retirement for just over a decade before passing away in 1893.

Think About This President and Prayer:
Garfield wanted people to know Jesus, not just know about Him. Do you know the difference?

Jesus isn't just someone who lived a long time ago. He's alive now and wants to have a personal friendship with you. How does that make you feel?

How to Pray Like James A. Garfield
"Lord Jesus, I am thankful for my faith in You, Your life, death and resurrection! I know, without a doubt, that You wait to welcome me to heaven if I will just believe in You. Help me to know You more deeply every day by talking to You and spending time in Your presence. Help me to live a life that shows what I believe about You. Amen."

Scripture
"Grace and peace be multiplied to you in the knowledge of God and of Jesus our Lord, as His divine power has given to us all things that pertain to life and godliness, through the knowledge of Him who called us by glory and virtue."
2 Peter 1:2–3

History
James A. Garfield was the last of the so-called "log cabin" presidents who were born on the frontier and worked their way up from the ranks of unskilled labor.

Another president who had won fame as a military leader, Garfield rose as high as Major General in the Army. In both his personal and professional life, Garfield had achieved great landmarks, and his term as president was no exception. Interestingly enough, Garfield was also the country's first left-handed president.

When he was young, he was "born-again" and his passion for Christ led him to seminary. He spent part of his life as a minister preaching revival messages.

As he attempted to board a train in early July, an angry attorney who had been denied a chance to become a judge shot the president. Although James Garfield seemed to recuperate well at first, he died at the New Jersey seashore on September 19, 1881.

James A. Garfield

BORN November 19, 1831, in Orange, Ohio
20TH PRESIDENT 1881

───────────── ★ ─────────────

James Garfield would listen to those around him, but he would rely on God as the ultimate source of wisdom.

"I shall greatly rely upon the wisdom and patriotism of Congress and of those who may share with me the responsibilities and duties of administration, and, above all, upon our efforts to promote the welfare of this great people and their Government I reverently invoke the support and blessings of Almighty God."
March 4, 1881—Inaugural Address

As a preacher he stood at the pulpit, thundering his message from the Word of God:

"…We not only declare our faith in the Christ of the past but in the present, who is alive forever more. Let me urge you to follow Him, not as the Nazarene, the Man of Galilee, the carpenter's son, but as the ever living spiritual person, full of love and compassion, who will stand by you in life and death and eternity."
—Sermon Preached by Rev. James Garfield Before Running for President

Chester A. Arthur

BORN October 5, 1829, in Fairfield, Vermont
21ST PRESIDENT 1881–1885

★

Chester A. Arthur entered his presidency struggling with how to help the nation come to grips with the loss of their leader. He told the people what he knew to be true, that God directs the paths of men and nations:

"Its harvests have been plenteous; its varied industries have thriven; the health of its people has been preserved; it has maintained with foreign governments the undisturbed relations of amity and peace. For these manifestations of His favor we owe to Him who holds our destiny in His hands the tribute of our grateful devotion...

To that mysterious exercise of His will which has taken from us the loved and illustrious citizen who was but lately the head of the nation, we bow in sorrow and submission."
December 6, 1881—First Annual Message

Think About This President and Prayer
Why do you think so many of our presidents gave God thanks for protecting and blessing our country?

How has God blessed you lately? Have you thanked Him?

How to Pray Like Chester A. Arthur
"In both good and bad times, Lord, I want to rely on You. At times when I have everything I want, and at times when I do not, I put my trust in You to provide. More than riches, fame or success, I want to be doing what You have planned for my life. Help me to know that plan and follow it. Amen."

Scripture
"Oh, taste and see that the LORD is good; blessed is the man who trusts in Him! Oh, fear the LORD, you His saints! There is no want to those who fear Him. The young lions lack and suffer hunger; but those who seek the LORD shall not lack any good thing."
Psalm 34:8–10

History
Some have labeled Chester A. Arthur as one of the "forgotten presidents." He came into the presidency in a less than ideal way, but Arthur left the White House with dignity and respect.

While his professional life may not have provided a perfect pedigree for the presidency, it did show an inkling of his character. Trained as a lawyer, Arthur's government service was by appointment rather than election. As a man and as a president, Arthur was incredibly honest in spite of the dishonest people around him.

Arthur was an honest and careful man, and he was careful to give the praise for successes where it was due: "The closing year has been replete with blessings, for which we owe to the Giver of All Good our reverent acknowledgment... for these and countless other blessings we should rejoice and be glad."

Against political advice, Arthur felt strongly that a huge tax surplus was an embarrassment to the government. When he tried to lower taxes to provide relief, Congress reacted by increasing the other tariffs.

As with past presidents, trying to keep from taking sides in party arguments and bring changes to government did not make him popular with other people in his party. As a result, Chester A. Arthur did not run for president again.

Think About This President and Prayer

President Cleveland said that if we look back, we can see times when God directed and protected our nation. What are the times in your past when God took care of you or your family?

God guides us in many ways. Sometimes He speaks through the Bible, and sometimes he speaks to our hearts and minds. How does God speak to you?

How to Pray Like Grover Cleveland

"Almighty God, I am humbled when I think of Your power and goodness. I thank You for the times when You have guided and protected me. I know I can trust You. I ask You to speak to me, and to those who lead our country. Show us the way to go and we will do great things in Your name. Amen."

Scripture

"For You will light my lamp; the LORD my God will enlighten my darkness. For by You I can run against a troop, by my God I can leap over a wall. As for God, His way is perfect; The word of the LORD is proven; He is a shield to all who trust in Him."
Psalm 18:28–30

History

Many presidents have served two times in a row, but Grover Cleveland was the only one to be president two different times. He was both the 22nd and 24th president.

In addition to that record, Cleveland set some other records while he lived in the White House. In 1886 he became the first president to be married in office when he chose a twenty-one-year-old bride. He also did unusual things such as naming his favorite guns and personally answering the White House phone. Cleveland was also the first president to appear in a photoplay (an early type of movie). It was called *A Capital Courtship* but it did not make President Cleveland a movie star!

The Washington Monument had just been built at the time when he became president, and the Statue of Liberty, a gift from France, was dedicated.

Cleveland didn't worry about being popular. He felt it was more important to stand for what you believe in. This conviction made him unpopular with many people. They didn't want to elect him. Cleveland argued back, "What's the point of being elected… unless you stand for something?"

After his second term as president, Cleveland retired to Princeton, New Jersey where he kept doing interesting things, just as he had in the White House, until he died in 1908.

Grover Cleveland

BORN March 18, 1837, in Caldwell, New Jersey
22ND & 24TH PRESIDENT 1885–1889 & 1893–1897

———————— ★ ————————

Grover Cleveland was a large man, but even he looked small standing in the shadow of the six-hundred-foot Washington Monument, as he uttered these words:

"Let us not trust to human effort alone, but humbly acknowledging the power and goodness of Almighty God, who presides over the destiny of nations, and who has at all times been revealed in our country's history, let us invoke His aid and His blessings upon our labors."
March 4, 1885—First Inaugural Address

When Cleveland was elected president for a second time, he spoke these words:

"Above all, I know there is a Supreme Being who rules the affairs of men and whose goodness and mercy have always followed the American people, and I know He will not turn from us now if we humbly and reverently seek His powerful aid."
March 4, 1893—Second Inaugural Address

Benjamin Harrison

BORN August 20, 1833, in North Bend, Ohio
23RD PRESIDENT 1889–1893

★

Benjamin Harrison told the nation that God is the source of our blessings:

"God has placed upon our head a diadem and has laid at our feet power and wealth beyond definition or calculation. But we must not forget that we take up these gifts upon the condition that justice and mercy shall hold the reigns of power and that the upward avenues of hope shall be free to all people."
March 4, 1889—Inaugural Address

When President Harrison wrote this speech, he turned the attention to his heavenly Father, instead of bragging about himself:

"Entering thus solemnly into covenant with each other, we may reverently invoke and confidently expect the favor and help of Almighty God—that He will give to me wisdom, strength, and fidelity, and to our people a spirit of fraternity and a love of righteousness and peace."

Think About This President and Prayer
What three things did Harrison ask God to give him?

What did he ask God to give the American people?

How to Pray Like Benjamin Harrison
"All I have comes from You, Father. I promise to show mercy to those around me. I will remember to show mercy and follow the truth every day. I ask You to give me wisdom and strength each day, that my life would be pleasing to You. Amen."

Scripture
"Let not mercy and truth forsake you; Bind them around your neck, write them on the tablet of your heart, and so find favor and high esteem in the sight of God and man."
Proverbs 3:3–4

History
Adding to the number of presidents born in Ohio, Benjamin Harrison won the presidency away from Grover Cleveland. He lost it back to him again four years later, however. You might have noticed that he has the same last name as a former president. That is because William Henry Harrison was his grandfather.

Harrison was not tall but he was known for being intelligent. He had a good education and had been a lawyer in Indiana. He ran for governor of Indiana, and then became a senator. Harrison had also served in the Civil War as a colonel in the infantry.

Harrison had many things going for him when he ran for re-election, but he lost. The reason was partly because of economic pressures and partly because of the popularity of Grover Cleveland. Upon his return to private life in Indianapolis, Harrison remarried and lived the next five years in retirement.

Think About This President and Prayer
Can you name a time when you felt so strongly about something that you had to repeat it, the way President McKinley repeated his promise to be a good president?

Why is it important to keep a promise?

How can God help you keep your promises?

How to Pray Like William McKinley
"Please forgive me, Father, for saying I love You once and then going about my life. While I may never make a promise as serious as the one to become the president, I still can repeat my promise to love You by my words and actions. You have promised to guide me for as long as I obey Your Word. Help me to obey You and to keep my promises. Amen."

Scripture
"Commit your way to the LORD, trust also in Him, and He shall bring it to pass. He shall bring forth your righteousness as the light, and your justice as the noonday."
Psalm 37:5–6

History
The past six elections had all been very close, but McKinley broke that pattern. He received most of the votes when he was elected.

Prior to the presidency, McKinley had imagined living a very quiet life. He started out in a career as a teacher in a local school. Then his life was changed when the Civil War broke out. He enlisted in the military as a private but he worked hard and was promoted again and again. William McKinley was promoted until he became a major.

Some people feel that the most important thing President McKinley did was not while he was in the United States, but while he was in other countries. He worked very hard to make Guam, Puerto Rico, and the Philippines become territories of the U.S.

In 1901, after winning election to a second term, McKinley was tragically shot while shaking hands with a crowd at the World's Fair in Buffalo, New York. A man who pretended to reach out to shake McKinley's hand fired two bullets from a gun wrapped in a handkerchief. McKinley was taken to the hospital, but died a few days later.

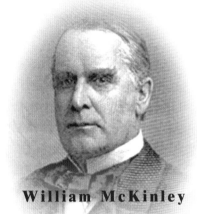

William McKinley

BORN January 29, 1843, in Niles, Ohio
25TH PRESIDENT 1897–1901

William McKinley promised to uphold the office of president with the newly invented motion picture camera recording his every move.

"I assume the arduous and responsible duties of president of the United States, relying upon the support of my countrymen and invoking the guidance of Almighty God. Our faith teaches that there is no safer reliance than upon the God of our fathers, who has so singularly favored the American people in every national trial, and who will not forsake us so long as we obey His commandments and walk humbly in His footsteps...I will faithfully execute the office of president of the United States, and will, to the best of my ability, preserve, protect, and defend the Constitution of the United States. This is the obligation I have reverently taken before the Lord Most High. To keep it will be my single purpose, my constant prayer..."
March 4, 1897 – First Inaugural Address

Theodore "Teddy" Roosevelt

BORN October 27, 1858, in New York, New York
26TH PRESIDENT 1901–1909

———————————— ★ ————————————

Teddy Roosevelt may not have looked like a person who studied a lot—most famous photos show him enjoying nature and sports. But he also loved to read and he honored the wisdom he gained from studying the Bible:

"Every thinking man, when he thinks, realizes that the teachings of the Bible are so interwoven and entwined with our whole civic and social life that it would be literally—I do not mean figuratively, but literally—impossible for us to figure what the loss would be if these teachings were removed. We would lose all the standards by which we now judge both public and private morals; all the standards towards which we, with more or less resolution, strive to raise ourselves."
Saturday, March 4, 1905—Inaugural Address

Think About This President and Prayer

In our country today, less and less people want to define right and wrong by what the Bible says. Can you think of something that the Bible says is wrong, but people today say is all right?

Have you ever been to another country? Even if you haven't, maybe you can think of some really good reasons to be thankful you live in America. What are they?

How to Pray Like Theodore Roosevelt

"Dear Lord, Your Word says, 'Blessed is the nation whose God is the Lord.' I thank You, Father, that I live in land where past leaders have done more than speak about You. They have let You lead them. Help our leaders to continue to follow Your voice when the troubles and needs of the world might try to distract them. May each leader be able to stand in front of this country and say, 'In God I Trust.' Amen."

Scripture

"The fear of the Lord is the beginning of wisdom, and knowledge of the Holy One is understanding."
Proverbs 9:10

History

Some of our presidents came into the office because they took over the job after the president in office died. Theodore Roosevelt was one of them—he became president after the death of William McKinley. "Teddy" Roosevelt worked hard to expand the powers of the presidency, also called the executive branch.

Roosevelt was born into a rich family in the East. He struggled with sickness throughout his life. There have been many rumors about Roosevelt's life, but one true story is that the stuffed children's toy—the 'Teddy Bear'—was named after him and his love for wildlife. He also established the idea of having national forests and parks because of his love of the great outdoors. Many of the great national parks we enjoy today are here because of Teddy Roosevelt's work.

Roosevelt did not seek a third term as president because he had promised not to do so. So in 1908, even though the economy was headed for the Great Depression and the country could have used an experienced leader, he stepped down. Since he had been the nation's youngest president up to that time, he was still active enough to enjoy travel and African safaris during his retirement.

Roosevelt traveled all over the world. He knew what he was talking about when he said, "...no people on earth have more cause to be thankful than ours, and this is said reverently, in no spirit of boastfulness in our own strength, but with gratitude to the Giver of Good who has blessed us with the conditions which have enabled us to achieve so large a measure of well being and of happiness."

Think About This President and Prayer

Can you name some times when you needed God's help to do something? Did you ask anyone to help you pray?

What might a president do differently if he asked for God's help?

How to Pray Like William Howard Taft

"Lord, I have a big job ahead of me. In a world filled with confusion I need to know You and Your truth. When I have doubts, please remind me that You are able to help me in any situation, no matter how big it may look. I thank You that You never change, even in the midst of my doubts. Amen."

Scripture

"Then Jesus said...'If you abide in My word, you are My disciples indeed. And you shall know the truth, and the truth shall make you free.'"
John 8:31–32

History

William Howard Taft was large in size and personality. Teddy Roosevelt chose Taft to follow him and run for president. Because they were so closely connected, many people can't think or talk about Taft's presidency without mentioning Roosevelt as well.

Surprisingly, being president was never something Taft had planned on doing. He was perfectly content to practice law and eventually became a judge.

In spite of the way he helped improve our government's economics, business relations and other areas, he did not win re-election. In fact, Taft came in last place of the three candidates who ran for president in 1912.

A short time later, Taft was appointed Chief Justice of the United States, a position he held for the remainder of his life. He considered that appointment to be his greatest achievement, even over the presidency. It had been his lifelong dream to be a Chief Justice. He enjoyed that post for almost a decade before dying in 1930.

William Howard Taft

BORN September 15, 1857, in Cincinnati, Ohio
27TH PRESIDENT 1909–1913

William Howard Taft watched the snow swirling that March morning as Inauguration Day progressed. Bundled against the cold, Taft left his breakfast with Teddy Roosevelt and walked toward the crowd. It was bitingly cold so the speech had been moved indoors. Taft spoke to the assembled crowd and at the end uttered this statement:

"I invoke the considerate sympathy and support of my fellow citizens and the aid of the Almighty God in the discharge of my duties."
March 4, 1909—Inaugural Address

Woodrow Wilson

BORN December 28, 1856, in Staunton, Virginia
28TH PRESIDENT 1913–1921

———————— ★ ————————

Woodrow Wilson was standing in drizzling rain, but he would not sit down until he finished what he had to say:

"America was born a Christian nation. America was born to exemplify that devotion to the elements of righteousness, which are derived from the revelations of Holy Scriptures. Ladies and Gentlemen, I have a very simple thing to ask of you. I ask of every man and woman in this audience that from this night on, they will realize that part of the destiny of America lies in their daily perusal of this great Book of Revelations. That if they would see America free and pure they will make their own spirits free and pure by this baptism of the Holy Scripture."
1911—Public Speech

Think About This President and Prayer
How different do you think our country would be if everyone studied the Bible every day and did what it says?

Why is wisdom the greatest thing a leader can ask God for?

How to Pray Like Woodrow Wilson
"Lord, we are Your people. Even though my country wants me to think I can believe in any religion, remind them of the ideas this country was built on. We are one nation under one God—You—and I ask that Your Spirit would flow into this country and into our lives to remind us of that. Give me the wisdom to do what is right each day, and to show Your glory in all I do. Amen."

Scripture
"If any of you lacks wisdom, let him ask of God, who gives to all liberally and without reproach, and it will be given to him."
James 1:5

History
It's hard to say whether Woodrow Wilson won his first presidential election because he was a good candidate or because his opponents were fighting with each other so much. Either way, Wilson won and was the first democratic president in the twentieth century.

Wilson's success was a surprise to many people. He had struggled with a learning disability that made reading hard for him. To make up for not reading well, he learned to remember everything even if he saw it only one time.

Under Wilson, the nation had to face a new idea—a war that involved the whole world. A war that started as "The War to End All Wars" instead became known as the first of two world wars.

Preoccupied by his wife's illness and death, World War I was easy for Wilson to avoid for the first few years. Although he tried to keep America out of the fight, by 1917 even he was ready to declare war on Germany.

Although almost all of the work to end the war was done by Wilson, his last term as president ended just a few short months before the peace process was completed.

Once he retired, he was able to recuperate from the stroke he suffered while championing the peace process. He retired to his home in the capital where he was nursed back to health by his second wife until he died five years later.

The Bible says that King Solomon asked for the greatest gift—wisdom. Woodrow Wilson asked for the same blessing so he could be a great national leader, too: "I pray God I may be given the wisdom and the prudence to do my duty in the true spirit of this great people."

Think About This President and Prayer
Imagine what it would feel like to have millions of people depending on you as the president of the United States. Have you prayed for our president today?

Do you think it is more powerful to quote the Bible, as President Harding did, rather than just talk about it?

How to Pray Like Warren G. Harding
"Dear Lord, when the world is too much for me to handle, help me to turn to You instead of away from You. Nothing I face in life is too big for You, God. Give me Your strength in the tough times and in the good times, too. You created me to walk through life with You, and I am amazed at Your great power and love. Amen."

Scripture
"My flesh and my heart fail; but God is the strength of my heart and my portion forever…it is good for me to draw near to God; I have put my trust in the Lord GOD, that I may declare all Your works."
Psalm 73:26, 28

History:
When bad things like wars happen, it usually makes people stop and think about what is really important. World War I caused many Americans to think about their lives and country in new ways.

Warren Harding finished the peace process that Wilson had started, and he believed that America needed a period of rest after the war. Harding didn't have to wonder if he had the support of Americans—six out of ten people had voted for him to become president in 1920.

As president, Warren Harding was the first president to be broadcast over the radio. In fact, he was the first president to even own a radio! Harding was also the first president to visit Canada and Alaska, and was the first to ride to his inauguration in the newly-invented automobile.

But Harding's time as president lasted only two years. The country lost another promising president much too soon when Harding suffered a heart attack and died on the way to California.

Warren G. Harding

BORN November 2, 1865, in Corsica, Ohio
29TH PRESIDENT 1921–1923

───────────── ★ ─────────────

When Warren G. Harding carried the weight of the most powerful country in the world on his shoulders, he turned to the One with strength to help him:

"Standing in this presence, mindful of the solemnity of this occasion, feeling the emotions which no one may know until he senses the great weight of responsibility for himself, I must utter my belief in the divine inspiration of the founding fathers. Surely there must have been God's intent in the making of this new-world Republic...I have taken the solemn oath of office on that passage of Holy Writ wherein it is asked: 'What doth the Lord require of thee but to do justly, and to love mercy, and to walk humbly with thy God?' This I [pledge] to God and country."
March 4, 1921—Inaugural Address

Calvin Coolidge

BORN July 4, 1872, in Plymouth, Vermont
30TH PRESIDENT 1923–1929

★

Calvin Coolidge believed that our country's motto should truly be "In God we trust," which is why he described the goals of our country this way:

"No ambition, no temptation, lures her to thought of foreign dominions. The legions which she sends forth are armed, not with the sword, but with the Cross. The higher state to which she seeks the allegiance of all mankind is not of human, but of Divine origin. She cherishes no purpose save to merit the favor of Almighty God."
March 4, 1925—Inaugural Address

Coolidge depended on the Word of God and his actions and words always brought God and government together…

"The foundations of our society and our government rest so much on the teachings of the Bible that it would be difficult to support them if faith in these teachings would cease to be practically universal in our country."

Think About This President and Prayer
Coolidge said that our armies have more power from the cross of Jesus than they have from weapons. How is the power of the cross stronger than the power of a weapon made by men?

Which earlier president also said that the teachings of the Bible are such an important foundation of our government that they can't be separated from it?

How to Pray Like Calvin Coolidge
"Each day, O Lord, I want to go out with Your words on my lips. Help me to boldly share with others the good news that You died on the cross to save us. The power of the cross is the true answer for our country's problems. Thank You that You have not separated Yourself from this country, even though foolish people in power have denied You. I thank You that some people in our government still believe in You. Give them strength and courage today. Amen."

Scripture
"For the message of the cross is foolishness to those who are perishing, but to us who are being saved it is the power of God."
1 Corinthians 1:18

History
Stepping in to fill the empty space left when Warren G. Harding died, Calvin Coolidge helped our nation. He had a spent a lot of time in public service, so he was ready for the highest office of the land—the office of president.

Coolidge jumped from state politics to national politics when he joined Harding as vice president. People liked him well enough to vote for him to stay in office when Harding's term was over. Coolidge proved he could handle the job of being president.

Amusingly, Coolidge liked simple ways, the kind of lifestyle people often have in the country or small towns. He felt that our whole country should live that way and slept eleven hours every night as an example to everyone.

This calm way of leading people made people in our nation happy. With more modern inventions, life was getting easier for most people and they didn't want a leader who would change that. Coolidge's years as president kept the happy lifestyle of Americans rolling along.

It surprised everybody when Calvin Coolidge asked thirty reporters to meet him in a high school classroom in South Dakota in 1927. At the meeting—called a press conference—he handed each reporter a slip of paper. The papers simply said that he would not run for president again.

Think About This President and Prayer
How do we allow bad influences and bad behavior to grow in our country?

Why do you think President Hoover thought these things were more dangerous than outside enemies?

How to Pray Like Herbert Hoover
"Please, God, help me never become numb to the evil things around me. Help me to remember that even though I must live in the world, it is not my true home. It is only a place that I pass through on my way to my real home in heaven with You. Help me shine a light in the darkness of this world through my actions. I need Your strength and blessing to live a life that is pleasing to You. Amen."

Scripture
"You are the light of the world....Let your light so shine before men, that they may see your good works and glorify your Father in heaven."
Matthew 5:14a, 16

History
It's easy to feel sorry for Herbert Hoover because a very hard time fell on our country while he was president. It was called "The Great Depression" and it was depressing!
Many people lost their jobs. People everywhere had little or no money. They had to travel long distances to find work so they could feed their families. Many families had to split up because they could no longer care for everyone. Even children went to work to get some extra money for their parents. It was hard for people to get used to going without the things they wanted after they had had so much fun during the 1920s.
How did these hard times start? When people buy stocks in companies, they keep track of those stocks in the stock market. If the stock market goes up, people make more money on their stocks. If the stock market goes down, people lose money. One day while Hoover was president, the stock market went so low, people say it crashed! This led into the Great Depression.
How much money did people lose? On the day that the stock market crashed, it lost almost as much money as it had taken to fight the entire First World War. That's a lot of money!
People everywhere were facing the hardest times ever, and President Hoover was stuck in the unwanted position of having to be their leader. People didn't really think it was his fault that their money was gone. But at re-election time, the American people did not vote for Hoover. They voted for Hoover's opponent and his programs that promised to help people get food and money until times got better.
After his term as president was over, Hoover served in other government positions, did some writing, and lived into the 1960s when he died at age ninety.

Herbert Hoover

BORN August 10, 1874, in West Branch, Iowa
31ST PRESIDENT 1929–1933

———————— ★ ————————

Herbert Hoover was getting ready for a big day. It's easy to imagine a crowd huddling close for warmth on a cold morning, waiting to hear what the new president had to say. They probably hoped Hoover would continue the 'roaring' lifestyle they had enjoyed under President Coolidge, but his statements show that he had some pretty traditional beliefs:

"It is a dedication and consecration under God to the highest office in service of our people. I assume this trust in the humility of knowledge that only through the guidance of Almighty Providence can I hope to discharge its ever-increasing burdens."

"Our strength lies in spiritual concepts. It lies in public sensitivities to evil. Our greatest danger is not from invasion by foreign armies. Our dangers are that we may commit suicide from within by complaisance with evil, or by public tolerance of scandalous behavior."
March 4, 1929—Inaugural Address

Franklin Delano Roosevelt

BORN January 30, 1882, in Hyde Park, New York
32ND PRESIDENT 1933–1945

★

Franklin Delano Roosevelt lay in a hotel bed in New York just after his election. He leaned through the darkness and told his son, Jimmy:

"I am afraid I may not have the strength to do this job. After you leave me tonight, Jimmy, I am going to pray… I hope you will pray for me, too."
1932—Biltmore Hotel in New York

After his two sons helped him walk to the platform, Roosevelt positioned himself before the crowd. Too proud to use a chair even though he was disabled, he told the nation…

"While this duty rests upon me I shall do my utmost to speak their purpose and to do their will, seeking Divine guidance to help us each and every one to give light to them that sit in darkness and to guide our feet into the way of peace."
January 20, 1937—Second Inaugural Address

Think About This President and Prayer

How is God's view of people with disabilities different from what other people might think about them?

Not everyone has a physical disability, but we all have strengths and weaknesses. Where are you weak? How does God help you become strong?

How to Pray Like Franklin Delano Roosevelt

"Heavenly Father, without You I am weak and worthless. Please be my source of strength, guidance, and peace. Let me be a light in the darkness to those who are far from You and an example to those who have turned their backs. I seek Your wisdom and direction for my life, my family and my nation. Amen."

Scripture

"And He said to me, 'My grace is sufficient for you, for My strength is made perfect in weakness.'…Therefore I take pleasure in infirmities, in reproaches, in needs, in persecutions, in distresses, for Christ's sake. For when I am weak, then I am strong."
2 Corinthians 12:9–10

History

Most people shorten his name to just his initials, FDR, but Roosevelt's presidency was not short. In fact, he was the only president to serve three terms in a row—that's twelve years. Roosevelt became president at a very important time for our country. Finances were very bad and Americans needed a leader who could help us out of the Great Depression. The people voted for Roosevelt because of his programs for food, money, and work. He called all of these programs the New Deal, and running them made him one of the most active presidents of all time.

At the time, most people did not know that FDR was disabled. A disease called polio had left him without the use of his legs, but FDR did not let that stop him. Knowing that Americans at that time were looking for a strong leader and might not vote for him if he seemed to have a physical weakness, he taught himself to "walk" without using his legs. Propping himself up between his sons he would grip their arms and move along with them.

Your grandparents can probably remember when our country was attacked by surprise during Roosevelt's presidency. On December 7, 1941, the Japanese attacked Pearl Harbor. President Roosevelt made a famous speech after the attack, assuring our country that the United States would not let our enemies take over. He rallied our nation and brought us into World War II.

FDR was a very important part of the leadership team who wanted to end World War II. He had many ideas that helped bring an end to the war, but he died unexpectedly on April 12, 1945, shortly before it ended.

Think About This President and Prayer

Have you ever needed God to help you know the difference between right and wrong? Why would a president need God's help to do this?

How different would our lives be if no one had ever fought to protect our freedoms? What are some things we might not be allowed to do?

How to Pray Like Harry S. Truman

"Dear Lord, You give me victory over my physical enemies, but more importantly, You give me victory over the devil. I thank You for both. For those who have laid down their lives in Your service or in the service of this country, I offer thanks. I know that many lives have been given so that I can live in freedom—including the freedom to worship You. I'm thankful that I've been blessed with freedom to worship You until I go to live in Your kingdom for all eternity. Amen."

Scripture

"But thanks be to God, who gives us the victory through our Lord Jesus Christ."
1 Corinthians 15:57

History

When asked about how FDR's death had changed him, Truman said that the "moon…stars…and planets had fallen" on him. Roosevelt had not always told Truman what was going on. When FDR died, Truman had a lot of catching up to do as he became the new president. It was important for him to know everything that was going on because of the very serious events that were taking place. It was the end of World War II.

One of the most dangerous things that Truman had not known about was the development of a new super weapon called the atomic bomb. After learning that our country had this weapon, he asked Japan to surrender. Truman used the atomic bomb twice and Japan agreed to peace, bringing World War II to an end.

The Truman years were very occupied with war, but they also built peace as he worked with the United Nations to write agreements that would help countries get along.

Yet Truman had scarcely seen the end of World War II when a struggle began raging in Korea. After almost two years embroiled in the Korean War, Truman made the decision not to run for another term as president. He lived out the reminder of his years in Independence, Missouri where he died almost thirty years after leaving office.

Harry S. Truman

BORN May 8, 1884, in Lamar, Missouri
33RD PRESIDENT 1945–1953

★

In his first speech to Congress, Harry S. Truman quoted the wisdom of King Solomon:

"At this moment I have in my heart a prayer. As I have assumed my heavy duties, I humbly pray, Almighty God, in the words of King Solomon: 'Give therefore thy servant an understanding heart to judge thy people, that I may discern between good and bad, for who is able to judge this thy so great a people?' I ask only to be a good and faithful servant of my Lord and my people."
April 16, 1945—Address Before Congress After the Death of FDR

After World War II ended, President Truman proclaimed a national day of prayer :

"I call upon the people of the United States…to unite in offering their thanks to God for the victory we have won, and in praying that He will support and guide us into the paths of peace."
August 16, 1945—Proclamation for Day of Prayer

Dwight D. Eisenhower

BORN October 14, 1890, in Denison, Texas
34TH PRESIDENT 1953–1961

President Eisenhower used Christian principles to outline his hopes for America when he added this prayer to his inaugural speech to the nation as president…

"Before all else, we seek, upon our common labor as a nation, the blessings of Almighty God. And the hopes in our hearts fashion the deepest prayers of our whole people.
May we pursue right—without self-righteousness.
May we know unity—without conformity.
May we grow in strength —without pride in self.
May we, in our dealings with all peoples of the earth, ever speak truth and serve justice."
January 21, 1957—Second Inaugural Address

Think About This President and Prayer
President Eisenhower said that the hopes in our hearts are like prayers. What hopes do you think people have that are like prayers?

If you are strong in something you do, can you be too proud of yourself?

How to Pray Like Dwight D. Eisenhower
"Please Lord, help me not to be proud of myself, but of what You have done for me. All my hope and confidence is in You. In each area, Lord, please grow me and mold me into the person You have longed to see. Let the people who live in this country be united in service to You no matter what other differences we may have. Amen."

Scripture
"Find rest, O my soul, in God alone; my hope comes from him. He alone is my rock and my salvation; he is my fortress, I will not be shaken."
Psalm 62: 5–6, NIV

History
Dwight D. Eisenhower was one of the strong presidents who came out of the military. The events of war forged within him a deep respect and appreciation of God. He demonstrated in his public life that the struggles he faced were no match for the Almighty: "In the swift rush of great events, we find ourselves groping to know the full sense and meaning of these times in which we live. In our quest of understanding, we beseech God's guidance."

He was nicknamed "Ike," and he brought the power and prestige of a battlefield hero to his presidency. A military man all of his life, Ike was the product of a West Point education and learned war administration while rising through the ranks of the army. He earned his general's stars while commanding the World War II forces in Africa and France.

Ike was preoccupied with domestic and international peace. He was not against using the threat of attack to achieve a peaceful result. While he cautioned against building military might to the point that it became a hazard to America's way of life, he urged that might is often necessary to protect peace.

Many of the key events that are still important in the U.S. today occurred during Ike's presidency. Russia's success in space and the tensions of the Cold War helped to create our own space program known as NASA. Suburban communities grew rapidly with the surge of affordable automobiles. The land changed greatly in just a generation of years previous.

Think About This President and Prayer

What does it mean to be a "citizen of America" and to be a "citizen of the world"?

How do you do God's work in America and the world?

How to Pray like John Fitzgerald Kennedy

"Some people turn from You, but please don't let me do so. Help me to speak out against those that deny You. I know that You are God and Your Son is my Savior. The standard of my life is to be a servant in Your sight. Let my life be tireless in Your service. Amen."

Scripture

"Speak up for those who cannot speak for themselves, for the rights of all who are destitute. Speak up and judge fairly; defend the rights of the poor and needy."
Proverbs 31:8–9, NIV

HISTORY

President Kennedy was both the youngest president elected and the youngest president assassinated. 'JFK' lived a long life in his few short years. His wife, Jackie, became an international influence in her own right. The Kennedy's seemed the ideal couple to govern a nation that saw itself at the forefront of everything.

In his time as president, Kennedy was concerned with domestic issues related to race and poverty. A tireless champion of the arts and culture, Kennedy's visions on everything from education to economics prompted people to respond. There was a feeling that the nation was on the right track. Internationally, Kennedy's short presidency saw some significant developments. Continuing the popular suspicion and rivalry with the communist countries, JFK would confront their 'evils' again and again.

While riding in a motorcade in Dallas, Texas on November 22, 1963, Kennedy was shot and killed. The untimely and tragic death of JFK imprinted itself on a nation and left the country shaken and in tears.

Kennedy lived at the time when a few powerful figures were winning the battle to shift the country's opinion away from God. These few, powerful and deceived officials chipped away at our Christian heritage tirelessly. For them America was a people whose rights were won by men, but for Kennedy there was no question about who really invested us with our inalienable rights:

"And yet the same revolutionary beliefs for which our forebears fought are still at issue around the globe – the belief that the rights of man come not from the generosity of the state, but from the hand of God."

John Fitzgerald Kennedy

BORN May 29, 1917, in Brookline, Massachusetts
35TH PRESIDENT 1961–1963

★

The temperature still below twenty-two degrees Fahrenheit and almost a foot of snow on the ground, many thought JFK would cancel the inaugural events. However that did not deter the young Kennedy. Standing before the assembled onlookers, this charismatic leader exhorted the crowd…

"Finally whether you are citizens of America or citizens of the world, ask of us the same high standards of strength and sacrifice which we ask of you. With a good conscience our only sure reward, with history the final judge of our deeds, let us go forth to lead the land we love, asking His blessing and His help, but knowing that here on earth God's work must truly be our own."
January 20, 1961—Inaugural Address

Lyndon Baines Johnson

BORN August 27, 1908, in Johnson City, Texas
36TH PRESIDENT 1963–1969

★

Lyndon Johnson felt the pressures of the presidency suddenly laid upon his shoulders. Echoing the profound words of a president long since past, Johnson said that the nation's legacy of presidential prayer is important. He wisely remembered:

"The men who have guided the destiny of the United States have found the strength for their tasks by going to their knees."

Standing before the nation as the new president in his own right, LBJ could take credit for his successes. Yet he was not so arrogant as to claim that he did so on his own. Instead he pointed the attention of the assembled crowd to a Higher Authority to which he pledged their services…

"My fellow countrymen, on this occasion, the oath I have taken before you and before God is not mine alone, but ours together."
January 20, 1964—Inaugural Address

Think About This President and Prayer
Have you ever made a promise to God along with your family or friends?

Do you think it would help to have a group all pray to keep a promise together?

How to Pray like Lyndon Baines Johnson
"Thank You, Lord, for prayer as a way to talk to You. Each time I am weak You make me strong. Each time I need direction, it is as close as a prayer to You. Forgive me for forgetting to pray more often and to thank You for caring about me. Amen."

Scripture
"Whoever confesses that Jesus is the Son of God, God abides in him, and he in God. And we have known and believed the love that God has for us. God is love, and he who abides in love abides in God, and God in him."
1 John 4:15–16

History
When the nation's leader changed from JFK to LBJ, the people were in for an unexpected change in many ways. At first the country was in shock from losing a popular young president. Lyndon Johnson was elevated to the White House in the worst possible way, so he had many things to overcome. Johnson tried to continue the policies and ideals of the Kennedy era. When it came time for re-election, the American voters sent Johnson to the White House in his own right by a landslide. Although some thought he was personally 'unlikable,' others felt that Johnson provided a sense of leadership that the nation craved.

Demonstrating power and energy, LBJ showed doubters his ability to push bills through Congress and get the job done. Sadly, whatever LBJ's successes or failures, they were all overshadowed by America's participation in a little Southeast Asian country named Vietnam. Although the nation had taken great strides at home and in space, social unrest, because of race and war tensions, took their toll causing Johnson to withdraw from the campaign of 1968. After leaving office and returning to Texas, Johnson died from a heart attack in 1973, just before the peace talks brought an end to the Vietnam War.

Think About This President and Prayer

When we ask for God's help in making decisions, who makes the final decision? Does God decide for us or help us to know right from wrong?

Can it be scary to do what God has shown you is the right thing? Can you think of some Bible stories about people who obeyed God when it was difficult?

How to Pray Like Richard Milhous Nixon

"We all have empty lives until we find Your purpose, Lord. Let me embrace that purpose, and let me work for You instead of my own goals. May I do everything for Your kingdom and Your will. Amen."

Scripture

"...he who sows to the to the Spirit will of the Spirit reap everlasting life. And let us not grow weary while doing good, for in due season we shall reap if we do not lose heart."
Galatians 6:8–9

History

Richard Nixon served as vice president under Eisenhower. He had to wait a little while for his time in the Oval office. His first priority was pulling U.S. troops out of Vietnam, then healing the rift at home that the conflict had caused. He wanted to promote peace in many places in the world. His accomplishments include negotiating peace in the Middle East and opening diplomacy with China. He promoted the space program and Neil Armstrong's 'one small step' onto the surface of the moon happened during his presidency. He won re-election by a huge margin of votes.

Unfortunately, one single event turned the nation's eye from Nixon's great accomplishments to a scandal. His Committee to Re-Elect the President (CREEP) used electronic listening devices to spy on his opponents in the Watergate Hotel. Richard Nixon was never directly implicated in the spying, but his refusal to turn over tapes that might show his activity looked suspicious. It angered the Congress and finally caused him to resign. Many were convinced that Nixon was an honorable man who made a series of bad choices.

Richard Milhous Nixon

BORN January 9, 1913, in Yorba Linda, California
37TH PRESIDENT 1969–1974

───────────── ★ ─────────────

Richard Nixon said that he felt the mission of America was to serve God:

"Let us pledge together to make these next four years the best four years in America's history, so that on its 200th birthday, America will be as young and as vital as when it began, and as bright a beacon of hope for all the world.

"Let us go forward from here confident in hope, strong in our faith in one another, sustained by our faith in God who created us, and striving always to serve His purpose."
January 20, 1973

Gerald R. Ford

BORN July 14, 1913, in Omaha, Nebraska
38TH PRESIDENT 1974–1977

★

After being nominated, Gerald Ford was humble, and remembered how prayer was important to his success:

"...I told my fellow countrymen, 'I am acutely aware that you have not elected me as your President by your ballots, so I ask you to confirm me as your President with your prayers.'

"On a marble fireplace in the White House is carved a prayer which John Adams wrote. It concludes, 'May none but honest and wise men ever rule under this roof.' Since I have resided in that historic house, I have tried to live by that prayer...

"My fellow Americans, I like what I see. I have no fear for the future of this great country. And as we go forward together, I promise you once more what I promised before: to uphold the Constitution, to do what is right as God gives me to see the right, and to do the very best that I can for America. God helping me, I won't let you down."
August 19, 1976—Republican Convention Speech

Think About This President and Prayer
President Ford talked about a prayer being carved on a White House fireplace. Whose prayer is it? Do you think it's a good prayer for our presidents and leaders to see often?

Does your school and local courthouse allow any prayers posted in their buildings?

How to Pray Like Gerald Ford
"Lord, in all things I acknowledge You and ask that that You would direct my path. In the time when I want to turn from Your will, please correct my steps and bring me back to You. In all things let me trust You and when others look at me let them see, not my strength or abilities, but instead, my reflection of You. Amen."

Scripture
"Trust in the LORD with all your heart, and lean not on your own understanding; In all your ways acknowledge Him, and He shall direct your paths."
Proverbs 3:5–6

History
"Jerry" Ford, as he was known, was something of a surprise to the notion of rule by popular consent. Although a fine president and a strong Christian, he was never elected. During the Nixon years, the vice president Spiro Agnew had resigned and Ford was appointed in his place. Thus, when Nixon resigned, Ford became president. He came into the Oval Office after a scandal in American politics. President Ford worked on ways to restore trust, so he could lead the nation.

Jerry Ford was the only president to have been an Eagle Scout. He was also a star athlete, and tried out for two National Football League (NFL) teams after college. At Yale he was both a coach and a law student. He served in Congress his entire public service career before heading to the White House. His reputation for integrity helped him as president. In fact, when Jimmy Carter took the oath of office he agreed with the popular sentiment that Ford had indeed worked hard to heal the country. Ford retired to Palm Springs, California with his wife, Betty.

Think About This President and Prayer

Jimmy Carter knew that George Washington had put his hand on a Bible when he had sworn the oath of office. Why is it important for Americans to remember our founding fathers' history?

Who gave President Carter the Bible he used himself for the oath of office? Has anyone given you a Bible? Have you ever given a Bible to anyone?

How to Pray Like Jimmy Carter

"Thank You, Lord Jesus, for coming to earth and dying for us. Let me not fear any evil that You have already defeated. Please help me to tell about You every day of my life. Amen."

Scripture

"He hath shewed thee, O man, what is good; and what doth the LORD require of thee, but to do justly, and to love mercy, and to walk humbly with thy God."

Micah 6:8, KJV

History

President Carter truly believed that a good man would succeed in Washington solely because he and his ideas were noble. He found out that the practical application of his honorable ideas were in difficult in Washington's political circles.

Trying to truly be a president of the people, Jimmy Carter conducted presidential activities in more simple ways. On Inauguration Day, he and his wife walked instead of riding in a limo. He would carry his own luggage on trips. But some jaded Washington leaders criticized Carter's simplicity as weakness.

Economic trouble in America caused Carter some struggles. A weakened economy and rising oil prices affected Americans in other ways besides high gasoline prices. Costs rose for heating, manufacturing, and defense. This caused economic problems for everyday people as well as businesses.

Not many public figures would appear on public television and profess faith in God. But Jimmy Carter was not afraid to take a stand for the truth:

"I believe, obviously, that Jesus is the Son of God, that He was the promised Messiah. I believe that He was born of the Virgin Mary. Those tenets of my faith are very secure for me...my religious faith is just like breathing for me, and it's hard for me to imagine if I didn't have any religious faith."

Carter's life after the presidency has been very active. He has represented the United States in world crises and his work developing Habitat for Humanity building program is well-respected. He has often been seen at Habitat construction sites with a hammer in his hand.

James Carter, Jr.

BORN October 1, 1924, in Plains, Georgia
39TH PRESIDENT 1977–1981

Jimmy Carter's hand touched the cracked leather of George Washington's Bible. He remembered that great presidents before him had used it:

"Here before me is the Bible used in the inauguration of our first President, in 1789, and I have just taken the oath of office on the Bible my mother gave me a few years ago, opened to a timeless admonition from the ancient prophet Micah: 'He hath shewed thee, O man, what is good; and what doth the Lord require of thee, but to do justly, and to love mercy, and to walk humbly with thy God.' (Micah 6:8)...

"And I join in the hope that when my time as your President has ended, people might say this about our Nation: that we had remembered the words of Micah..."

January 20, 1977—Inaugural Address

Ronald Reagan

BORN February 6, 1911, in Tampico, Illinois
40TH PRESIDENT 1981–1989

★

President Reagan shared this at the National Prayer Breakfast in the ballroom of the Washington Hilton:

"I've always believed that we were, each of us, put here for a reason, that there is a plan, somehow a divine plan for all of us. I know now that whatever days are left to me belong to Him.

"I also believe this blessed land was set apart in a very special way, a country created by men and women who came here not in search of gold, but in search of God. They would be free people, living under the law with faith in their Maker and their future.

"Sometimes, it seems we've strayed from that noble beginning, from our conviction that standards of right and wrong do exist and must be lived up to. God, the source of our knowledge, has been expelled from the classroom. We...turn away from Him too often in our day-to-day living. I wonder if He isn't waiting for us to wake up..."

February 4, 1982—Annual National Prayer Breakfast

Think About This President and Prayer
Why is it important to search to know God more than gold or other riches?

If public schools do not allow students to pray aloud, how could the kids there still serve God each day at school?

How to Pray Like Ronald Reagan
"Heavenly Father, I know You have set each of us apart for great things. Help me to bring others to know Your Son. I'm thankful that I can serve You. Thank You for freedom for my country and for freedom for my soul. I commit this day to following You. Amen."

Scripture
"...call upon Me and go and pray to Me, and I will listen to you. And you will seek Me and find Me, when you search for Me with all your heart."
Jeremiah 29:12–13

History
Ronald Reagan was called the 'Great Communicator' because he had polished his speaking skills during his acting career. He had been in over fifty-three films, many times as the star. Reagan was a popular man who knew how to use words effectively. When he was hired to be a spokesman for General Electric Company, Reagan began to be more interested in politics. He earned a reputation as an engaging public figure in California and was elected the governor of that state. He began voting as a member of the Democratic Party, but changed sides to become one of the strongest leaders of the Republican Party.

Once he had attained the highest office of the land, Reagan led the way to stability by lowering taxes, building the military, and increasing employment. The nation rallied around him sending him back to the White House in 1984 by a clear majority. Even though very popular, he was shot by a deranged man less than three months after entering office. His quick recovery and public strength confirmed to the nation that they had made the right choice. He said, "I'm convinced more than ever that man finds liberation only when he binds himself to God and commits himself to his fellow man."

Following his years as president, Ronald Reagan stayed on the nation's radar as a public figure. Sadly those appearances declined as he became more debilitated from Alzheimer's disease. He and his wife, Nancy, retired in California.

Think About This President and Prayer
What is power? What did Jesus do with His power?

President Bush said he we should use power to serve others. What else might someone do with power?

How to Pray Like George H. W. Bush
"In the times when I feel that I have nowhere else to turn, thank You, Lord God, that I can go to You in prayer. You are the most powerful source of strength. Help me to come to You instead of trying to "tough out" my life's battles on my own. Thank You for leaders who are still led by Your hand. I pray for Your continued blessing over this nation and those that lead her. Amen."

Scripture
[Jesus said,] "I am the good shepherd. The good shepherd lays down his life for the sheep."
John 10:11, NIV

History
The initials 'H. W.' were added when using George Bush's public name when his son George W. Bush was elected the 43rd president of the United States. George H. W. Bush became president after one unsuccessful 1980 election campaign and after eight years as Reagan's vice president. President Reagan's election seemed to show the nation's hopes for a new direction. President Bush's election showed that most people hoped that the new direction would continue.

George Bush had a very interesting career in government service. He went from a seat in Congress, to a post as an ambassador, to the director of the Central Intelligence Agency (CIA) before serving under Reagan. Before that, Bush was the winner of the Distinguished Flying Cross as a pilot in the navy. In fact, he can be seen on video being rescued by a submarine from his downed airplane.

The Bush years saw some of the most incredible shifts in world power. The Soviet Union finally collapsed and the Berlin Wall came down. To many, the fall of that wall symbolized that the world had finally progressed past an era of fear and danger from nuclear war. As the more dangerous nations of the world tried to flex their muscle, Bush held them back. During the Gulf War, George Bush successfully defended the nation of Kuwait from Saddam Hussein. His troops so thoroughly routed the enemy that the ground war was won in just over one hundred hours. His popularity after this event did not gain him re-election 1992, however. He and his wife, Barbara, retired in Texas.

George H.W. Bush

BORN June 12, 1924, in Milton, Massachusetts
41ST PRESIDENT 1989–1993

George H.W. Bush set his priorities for the nation within the first sixty seconds of his term by telling the waiting crowd:

"…And my first act as President is a prayer. I ask you to bow your heads:

"Heavenly Father, we bow our heads and thank You for Your love. Accept our thanks for the peace that yields this day and the shared faith that makes its continuance likely. Make us strong to do Your work, willing to heed and hear Your will, and write on our hearts these words: 'Use power to help people.' For we are given power not to advance our own purposes, nor to make a great show in the world, nor a name. There is but one just use of power, and it is to serve people. Help us to remember it, Lord. Amen."
January 20, 1989—Inaugural Address

William Jefferson Clinton

BORN August 19, 1946, in Hope, Arkansas
42ND PRESIDENT 1993–2001

★

Near the end of his presidency, Bill Clinton found that he could no longer deny embarrassing things he had done in office. At the annual prayer breakfast in Washington, D.C., he had a look of remorse in his eyes when he made a request of forgiveness to the ministers and fellow Christians who had supported him as their nation's leader. He looked toward them and offered this plea:

"I ask you to share my prayer that God will search me and know my heart, try me and know my anxious thoughts, see if there is any hurtfulness in me, and lead me toward the life everlasting. I ask that God give me a clean heart, let me walk by faith and not sight."
September 11, 1998—Annual Prayer Breakfast

Think About This President and Prayer
Some religions do not teach that there is such a thing as sin. What does the Bible teach?

When we know we have sinned, what does the Bible tell us to do?

How to Pray Like William Jefferson Clinton
"Please forgive me for the times when I fail You, God. Help those around me to give me compassion and forgiveness. Help me to also forgive others. Thank You that in all things the blood of Jesus stands ready to cover over each sin if I will just ask. For all our presidents who try to follow You, I ask for Your mighty power to flow over their lives and build them up as strong instruments for You. Amen."

Scripture
"Search me, O God, and know my heart; test me and know my anxious thoughts. See if there is any offensive way in me, and lead me in the way everlasting."
Psalm 139:23–24, NIV

History
Sadness was cast over his presidency by the various scandals that arose during his time in office. He was elected as a symbol of America's hope for prosperity and growth. In some ways he did deliver that expectation as the economy grew.

He was born just three months after his father died in a car crash. Bill Clinton had a less then ideal start to life. Not one to be stopped from excellence, he did quite well in academics eventually ending up as a Rhodes Scholar at Oxford. He went to law school at Yale and returned to Arkansas to enter politics.

Some observed that governing the nation was what Clinton did between meetings with his lawyers because of so many rumors and court hearings. Stories of his personal activities shook the confidence of a nation. Many felt the choices that he made in office were understandable because of the lack of moral values of our time. Many disagreed and felt his actions were not excusable. But in the end, President Clinton himself asked for forgiveness, not excuses. He met privately with ministers expressly invited for the purpose of improving his walk with God. A nation saw their leader's public acceptance of his own errors and thousands remembered him in prayers during his public struggle with personal troubles.

Think About This President and Prayer
What is patience? Have you ever been patient?

How does President Bush say that we can feel comfort when we are sad?

How to Pray Like George W. Bush
"In moments of sorrow, O Lord, I ask that You will give me Your joy. In moments of distress, I pray for Your strength. In moments of unspeakable tragedy I rest in Your continued guidance and power. Help me not to let events in this world shake my belief in You. In all things, good and bad, let me to look to You. May each and every day be dedicated in thought and action to You, Lord Jesus. Amen."

Scripture
"For I am convinced that neither death nor life, neither angels nor demons, neither the present nor the future, nor any powers, neither height nor depth, nor anything else in all creation, will be able to separate us from the love of God that is in Christ Jesus our Lord."
Romans 8:38–39, NIV

History
Although he was the winner of one of the most contested elections in American history, George W. Bush followed in the footsteps of his father to become the nation's president. He rallied an entire country through some difficult times and restored respect for the office of the president. Following a leader who many felt did not respect the moral duties of the office, George W. Bush has been very public about his faith and that he goes to God for wisdom and strength.

Within months of his inauguration, George W. Bush was confronted with one of the most spectacular displays of evil this world has ever seen. On September 11, 2001, the nation, and indeed the world, watched with horror as fanatics turned planes, filled with innocent civilians, into flying missiles and forever changed the landscape of New York City. The event reached past New York, to the Pentagon, the fields of Pennsylvania, into every firehouse and police station in the world and into the everyday lives of ordinary people who had to confront their pain and sorrow caused by these events.

George W. Bush appeared as a calm and strong rallying point for the country. We each remember where we were as the Towers came down and many remember seeing the normally unshakable visage of Dan Rather lost for words near the edge of tears. And many remember where we were when George W. Bush promised to find and punish those who would do such a horrible thing. George W. Bush has continued to make good on that promise and brought a measure of safety back to America.

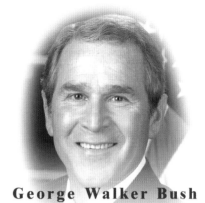

George Walker Bush

BORN July 6, 1946, in New Haven, Connecticut
43RD PRESIDENT 2001–

After the sorrow of September 11, 2001, George Bush spoke and prayed:

"There are prayers that help us last through the day, or endure the night...that give us strength for the journey... that yield our will to a will greater than our own.

"This world He created is of moral design. Grief and tragedy and hatred are only for a time. Goodness, remembrance, and love have no end. And the Lord of life holds all who die, and all who mourn...

"America is a nation full of good fortune...But we are not spared from suffering...On this national day of prayer and remembrance, we ask Almighty God to watch over our nation, and grant us patience and resolve in all that is to come. We pray that He will comfort and console those who now walk In sorrow. We thank Him for each life we now must mourn, and the promise of a life to come.

"As we have been assured, neither death nor life, nor angels nor principalities nor powers, nor things present nor things to come, nor height nor depth, can separate us from God's love. May He bless the souls of the departed. May He comfort our own. And may He always guide our country. God bless America."

September 14, 2001—National Day of Prayer & Remembrance